ANA L. FLORES & ROXANA A. SOTO

BILINGUAL *is* **Better**

TWO LATINA MOMS ON HOW THE
BILINGUAL PARENTING REVOLUTION IS CHANGING
THE FACE OF AMERICA

BiLiNGUAL
READERS

Published in the United States by Bilingual Readers
www.bilingualreaders.com | www.bilingualreaders.es
twitter.com/BilingualRdrs
facebook.com/bilingualreaders

First Edition: September 2012
ISBN: 9788492968213
Also available as an e-book: 9788492968220

Printed in the United States of America

DL: M-24257-2012

To my husband, José, for believing in this project as much as me, and to Vanessa and Santiago, our two best creations. But mostly to mis padres, *Miguel and Gloria, the original architects of my bilingual and bicultural journey.*

ROXANA A. SOTO

To my mami *for being responsible of my bilingualism (and so much more!). To my* papi *for my bicultural life. To Alan for his eternal patience, support and solid love. To my girl,* por ser mi inspiración y motivación constante.

ANA L. FLORES

Contents

Contents

Foreword

＊

OFTEN WE DON'T WANT TO BE LIKE OUR PARENTS. HOWEVER, THERE is one thing I want to do exactly like my parents did. They gave me the gift of being raised bilingual. I was born in Texas to Chilean parents and, once we moved to Chile when I was seven, I attended an American school. At home we always spoke the language that was not spoken primarily in school so we could keep the second language alive. It was challenging for my parents and for my brother and I. For my parents, English was not a native tongue and it wasn't easy to speak it fluently. For me, Spanish presented its own challenges, especially when I had to write it. I still remember the hours I spent with a tutor that first year in Chile so I could learn grammar and spelling. Ironically, most of my life I have made a living thanks to my Spanish writing skills.

During our summer vacations, we practiced our English thanks to yearly visits to the United States. There were no tablets, e-books, apps or websites, so we would actually spend a healthy dose of money on books and magazines which I took back to Chile and reread countless times over the year.

Now that I am a mother, I am doing everything I can to bestow the same gift my parents gave me upon my children. Since we proudly live in the United States, we predominately speak Spanish at home. It gets harder and harder each year, since my son and daughter prefer to speak English amongst themselves. This English dominance gets stronger the longer they spend in school, and the more friends they have. Once a year we try to travel as a family to Chile, so they can practice their Spanish and learn about different customs and cultures.

No matter how difficult it might seem at times, I believe this is a battle worth fighting. Even if I am sometimes so tired I don't want to answer in Spanish or make my children re-phrase what they said in English. I not only want my children to learn Spanish; I want them to be truly bilingual and fluent in both languages and, hopefully, both cultures.

For reasons I cannot quite understand, many do not see speaking more than one language as an advantage. They actually see it as a threat. I can only see advantages. Speaking English and Spanish since I can remember has allowed me to grow in different countries, work in diverse environments, and expand the boundaries of the life I live.

Aside from the scientific advantages of being bilingual, which this book's authors expose so well, I strongly believe in the social and cultural benefits of speaking more than one language.

Curiously, my parents did not do as their parents or grand-parents had done. My great grandparents were Ukrainian and Romanian immigrants that ended up in South America, yet none of their descendants learned their native languages. They wanted their children to fit in. So in their new countries, Argentina and later Chile, Spanish was the language they all learned.

That mission, to fit in, was accomplished but at the cost of severing all ties to their country of origin. I remember when I was seven or eight I would go to my grandfather and beg him to teach me a few words in Russian (at that time, I did not understand the difference between Russia and Ukraine, both were simply part of the Soviet Union). I did not believe him when he said he did not know any.

I've also seen this in some parts of the United States. Families that have Hispanic surnames but decided that if their children were to fit in this country, they needed to only speak English. Speaking even a word of Spanish could be grounds for punishment.

Today, for many, that is beyond comprehension because we like to believe we live in a more tolerant, sophisticated world. However, this is not necessarily true. In some cities, there is more tolerance for different accents, countries of origin and languages. In others, we still have a long way to go.

Personally, I cannot understand why we can't teach our children more languages aside from English. European children are exposed to different languages since they're preschoolers and it is not uncommon for them to have mastered three, four or even more languages by the time they graduate high school. Their loyalty to their country of origin is never disputed. Their cultural identity is not in peril. So, why do some keep insisting we should not teach more languages to our children?

This book comes at the perfect time to open up the conversation about the type of education we want for our children, how we can educate them, how we intend to broaden our horizons even if it means an extra effort for us as parents. That is why the entire premise is that bilingual is better for our children.

In this book you will not only learn about the scientific evidence that supports the benefits of raising bilingual children. With her journalistic background, Roxana Soto is used to reporting the facts. When combined with Ana Lilian Flores' bilingual upbringing and experience as a communicator, the perspective they share on bilingualism is enlightening. Plus, both of them are moms and have constantly interacted online through their website SpanglishBaby with a growing community of parents who want to raise their children to be able to combine both languages and not have to sacrifice one over the other.

To those who say it's impossible, I am living proof that they are wrong.

I hope this book inspires you to support bilingual education. Or at least, it starts the conversation. Because even if you have not considered or have a negative view of teaching more than one language to your child, you will read about different points of view that will give you plenty of perspective on the debate.

And to Ana and Roxana, once again I thank you for honoring me with this foreword to your new baby. You are a constant inspiration not only to me but to thousands of parents all over the world.

JEANNETTE KAPLUN
Journalist, international TV co-host,
author, and co-founder of Todobebé

Introduction

＊

W̲E ALWAYS GET ASKED HOW AND WHY WE GOT STARTED with SpanglishBaby the blog. The idea was conceived in the summer of 2008 because we were looking for Spanish children's books online and we couldn't really find any. A bit more research proved that, in fact, there weren't a lot of resources in general out there for Latino parents who, like us, wanted to raise bilingual and bicultural children.

Neither one of us really knew much about blogging, but with many years of experience in other types of media —including television and newspapers—behind us, the Internet seemed like the next logical step for two stay-at-home first time moms. One thing we did know was that we wanted our daughters to not only speak our native Spanish, but also to be as immersed in their Latino heritage as possible.

It took us about six months to figure out the technical aspects of blogging and to create enough content to feel comfortable putting our site out there for everyone to see. In February 2009, we launched SpanglishBaby and we were amazed to see how quickly we got a positive response from a community of parents who shared our views. It seemed as if they had been looking for a place to go to with their questions and doubts, but more than anything, for a community where they could share their stories about the trials and triumphs of raising children in two languages and two cultures in the United States today.

This book is an extension of our blog and in it we hope to convey the same familiar and inviting feeling we've been able to nurture online for the past three and a half years. There are already several well-written books on the mechanics of raising bilingual children, so you won't really find a lot of that here. What you will find are the very real experiences of two Latina moms—who've been very close friends since college (back in the 90s)—who need to make sure their children never forget where they came from.

ANA'S STORY

I've never been good with labels. They pin you down to one existence, to one experience. But there's one label I cannot escape: *Mamá.*

I am a *Mamá* and a Mom. I am also a bicultural and bilingual woman.

How I came to own those labels is part of my life story, which is defined by experiences that were predestined for me.

Destiny had it that my mom and dad, both born and raised in El Salvador, would start their very young marriage by relocating to Houston, Texas. *Mis abuelos,* using their political and military influence (both my grandfathers were high-ranking officials and diplomats), managed to get my dad hired at the Salvadoran consulate in Houston.

Two years later—in 1972—, I was born a U.S. citizen and baptized Ana Lilian Flores Martínez, after my *mami.* Not even three weeks after I was born, I got my first taste of my destiny as a bicultural child. My maternal *abuela,* Irma, decided her first granddaughter needed to make her debut in El Salvador as soon as possible. My newborn self was quickly put on a plane and taken to the country I would years later consider my home.

The first six years of my life in Houston were spent living in Spanish and English. Spanish was the language of home, of *familia*, of my *nana* and *amigos*. English was the language of my neighbors, my TV shows, my preschool, my kindergarten.

I clearly remember owning a kid's plastic album player, *un tocadiscos*, and playing a Cri Cri vinyl over and over. Until one day, when my fraternal *abuela*, Berta, came to visit and accidentally sat on it. I was as destroyed as the album was. In pieces. This was the 70s, when things were really valuable because they were not easily replaced, especially not a Spanish Cri Cri album in Houston! I think I can label this experience as my first huge dissapointment in life.

Little did I know that the dissapointment of losing my Cri Cri album wouldn't compare to that of my parents divorcing when I was six years old. Honestly, I'm assuming I was destroyed. I mean, I had to have been, right? I really don't remember a thing. No fights, no moments of recognition that something was wrong. They were either really good at hiding it from my little sister and I or I've just deleted it from my memory.

What I do remember is all those road trips we used to take from Houston to El Salvador to visit *familia*. I have memories of the most beautiful pink sunrises on the road. But the trip that is most stuck in my mind is when we moved and did the road trip without *mi papá*. My warrior mom took her two girls, my *tía* (her sister) who was only eighteen, and her best friend with her daughter on a trip across three borders aboard two cars—a van and a new Mustang— filled to the brim and brand new appliances to sell in El Salvador and start our new life.

That new life was spent in El Salvador attending the American School, protected in the capital city from the civil war that raged until 1991, and traveling every year with my sister to spend summers at our dad's house in Houston.

In El Salvador, our life was surrounded by servants and leisure, but in Houston we had to learn to do all our chores and not complain about a thing. I absorbed everything and learned to easily flow between the nuances of both cultures, ultimately choosing to move back to the United States for college. When asked "Where are you from?" I always reply "El Salvador," but the United States is where I've now chosen to call home and raise my daughter. I will forever live with *un pie aquí y otro allá*, now even more so for the sake of my girl.

I love having had the gift of innate bilingualism and a seamless bicultural upbringing. Although my girl's life circumstances are not the same as mine, my husband (born and raised in Mexico) and I have chosen to make a conscious effort to help her grow up as close as possible to her Mexican, Salvadoran and American roots and the language that binds us all together: Spanish. Our hope is that by gifting her with a second language at home she will never feel like a stranger when she travels to visit her *familia*. Language and a love for her heritage will instantly bind her to them. And that is what my personal mission with SpanglishBaby, both the online site and this book, is all about.

ROXANA'S STORY

One lone, framed photograph sits on my desk in my home office in the suburbs of Denver. It shows a beaming ten-year-old me gloriously standing in front of my Dad's beloved rose garden at our home in South Africa. I'm in full regalia: my Catholic school's maroon formal uniform, which included a coat and a tie! On my lapel, a big white badge with the word MERIT printed in black. My proud father took the picture back in the winter of 1983, immortalizing the momentous milestone in my short life when my bilingual journey took off.

A native Spanish speaker born in Peru and raised by bilingual (Spanish/English) parents, I had been exposed to English only sporadically in my first decade of life, so when we moved to Johannesburg, English was not my forte. A few months of immersion in my second language, however, did the trick. The merit badge—a monthly recognition awarded to the best student in my class—was proof. I keep the photograph on my desk as a reminder of the role bilingualism has played in my life and the rewards I've received because of it.

The tale of how I grew up bilingual and bicultural is totally different from that of my children or, for that matter, that of my parents—both of whom were born and raised in Peru. My mother had the good fortune—and a visionary father—to go to a private British school where she was instructed mainly in English. Although self-taught, my dad's English was impeccable, particularly when it came to grammar—many times rivaling those who spoke it as their first language. For my parents, being bilingual was the tool for getting ahead in life by providing them with more professional opportunities than the monolinguals around them.

My dad's bilingualism opened a series of doors for him, which had us traveling to different countries where he was transferred, not only for his professional expertise, but also for his mastery of English, the international language of business. Before I turned fifteen, I had lived in five countries on three continents—Peru, Mexico, Argentina, South Africa and the United States—and had been exposed to at least four languages: Spanish, English, French and Afrikaans.

I cannot deny that moving every couple of years was a bit rough growing up, but I would not change it for the world. While the constant relocations meant leaving friendships behind, they also meant we got to meet people from all kinds of backgrounds, expanding our understanding of diversity like no other experience could have done.

By the time my father was transferred to Florida, I had had several years of solid dual language instruction in English and Spanish (at the same private British school my mom attended as a child). Although moving to the United States as a teenager was a shock, being proficient in the majority language made a huge difference. At least I could communicate. But because I was not happy with our latest international move, I rebelled by befriending as many other Spanish speakers as possible. Luckily for me, we lived in Miami. I remember how I yearned for Peru—where we had settled after our short stint in South Africa—and I felt as if refusing to embrace my new life would make my parents feel guilty for yanking me out of school and separating me from my friends at the crucial age of fourteen.

As destiny would have it, however, our relocation to Miami would be our last international move. Though it took me a while to accept it, I eventually came to terms with my new reality: I was part of the rapidly growing number of Latinos trying to maintain our rich heritage while carving out a new life in the United States. A tall order for sure, especially once I became a mother.

The story of how my daughter and my son are growing up to be bilingual and bicultural is completely different than my own story because they are first generation Americans born to immigrant parents who moved to this country as teenagers. My husband and I are at ease in both the American and the Latino cultures as well as in English, Spanish and Spanglish—which we define as the ability to switch back and forth between both our languages without even noticing. We're both bilingual journalists who have spent a good amount of time working in the Spanish language media so we don't live in English or in Spanish. We live in both. Every day. All day long, except in front of our kids.

When I married my Puerto Rican husband, whose first language is Spanish, there was never a doubt in our minds that our children's first language would be Spanish, too. In fact, it was a topic we never even discussed because speaking Spanish to our children is the *only* natural way for us to communicate with them. Spanish is our language of love. Having lived the professional advantages of bilingualism, I know first hand the power of speaking more than one language. Yet, to me, those are added benefits. Speaking Spanish to my children is about cultural identity. It's about *familia*. It's a matter very close to my heart.

Writing this book—while working a full-time job, nurturing and growing SpanglishBaby and raising two children under the age of six—has been one of the most challenging tasks I've ever undertaken. But because I strongly believe in the power behind bilingualism and I am so intent on teaching others about it, all the sleepless nights and endless editing sessions have been well worth it. I hope you think so too and find in here all the information necessary to convince you to join us in our quest to take this bilingual parenting revolution to new heights, so that all children—regardless of where they come from or what they look like—can reap the benefits of speaking more than just one language.

As a journalist and a long time lover of the written word, writing a book has always been one of my dreams. Truthfully, I never imagined it would be about this topic. Not when I was growing up bilingual nor when we launched SpanglishBaby the blog. Either way, I couldn't be more ecstatic that

I've been given the opportunity to share what I know about something I'm so passionate about.

My only regret, as I sit here tweaking the last few details, is that my father, one of the precursors to my own family's bilingual journey, will not be here to read it. He died in 2004. I don't think he ever imagined, not in a million years, that his unrelenting determination to teach himself a second language as a means to excel in his professional career was such an extremely powerful way of showing my siblings and I that the sky is the limit for bilinguals. I'm here today, introducing you to my very first book, to prove it. And for that, I will be forever grateful to *mi padre.*

HOW TO READ THIS BOOK

While we would be happiest if you read our book in chronological order from beginning to end, we've actually written it in a way that allows you to pick it up whenever you like and start reading whatever tickles your interest at that specific time. In other words, if all you want to read about is bilingual education, all you have to do is turn to chapter 4. Within each chapter, you'll also find subheadings, which we hope will make it easier to navigate the content according to what you feel like reading about at any given moment. So, for example, if you're only interested in reading about how bilingualism is better for your child's brain, just go to chapter 2 and look for that heading.

Also, while the title of this book is *Bilingual is Better,* and the majority of its content attempts to explain why we believe that is true, we do spend a considerable amount of space talking about biculturalism, as we believe that raising bilingual children goes hand in hand with raising them to be bicultural. After all, one of the best ways to expose your children to their minority or heritage language is through culture: music, food and traditions.

WHO SHOULD READ THIS BOOK?

We wrote this book with a variety of people in mind. From other bilingual Latino parents who, like us, want to make sure to pass their heritage—and native tongue—on to the next generation to the many monolingual American parents who are starting to realize why they should raise their children to be bilingual and everyone in between, we believe there's something for everyone in this book. If you are interested in the benefits of bilingualism, in chapter 2 you will find a plethora of recent studies, which will serve as proof that you've made the right choice by deciding to raise bilingual children. If you, on the other hand, are on the fence about raising your children with more than one language because you've heard a lot of the same old myths surrounding this topic, the information in chapter 2 will also hopefully help to convince you to take the plunge.

For those of you who are bilingual and have lived between two worlds and in two cultures like we have, we imagine you're going to see yourself a lot in the pages of our book. But even if you don't share this background with us, you'll find a lot of practical advice—and real life stories—throughout the book on how to raise bilingual children even if you're not bilingual yourself. In the end, it is our genuine hope that, if nothing else, our book serves as proof that there's nothing weird about speaking a second language and that just because bilinguals in the United States speak more than just English doesn't mean they're not American enough.

The New Face of America

ROXANA A. SOTO

✳

W HEN WE LAUNCHED SPANGLISHBABY IN THE WINTER OF
2009 and I shared the blog with my family back
in Peru, I particularly remember the response
from one of my aunts. While she praised the
site for its content and design, she genuinely wondered
why there would be a need for something like it. After all,
a bilingual mother herself, she had raised two bilingual children in Mexico without many of the worries we seemed to
be concerned with in the blog: "Is one method better than
the other? How can we make sure our kids learn to read and
write correctly in Spanish? What if they refuse to speak the
minority language?" The answer to my aunt's question was
obvious. While we rave about the intellectual advantages of
raising bilingual children, for many of us it's also the best way
to make sure that our Hispanic heritage lives on.

My aunt didn't have to worry about this while she was raising
my cousins bilingually because they were immersed in Mexican
culture by virtue of where they lived. So the determination of
Latinos in the United States to preserve our cultural heritage
is a foreign concept to her. It's also something lots of people in
this country—who firmly believe that all immigrants, regardless
of their country of origin, have to assimilate into American culture—don't understand and therefore reject. While all Americans, with the exception of Native Americans, were immigrants
at some point, most haven't maintained the culture, traditions

or native languages of their ancestors, preferring instead to just blend into the melting pot that is the United States.

But why should we have to choose one over the other? I believe you can be perfectly American and still honor your ancestors' heritage because if you don't know where you came from, how can you possibly know where you're going? Our culture, our traditions, our language are the foundations upon which we build our identity. Speaking Spanish, then, shouldn't have to mean that you're being disloyal to the United States—as many people have claimed—it's just a way to keep the connection to our roots and to our *familia* back in Latin America alive.

This, however, is something you only understand if you are Latino. But what does that term really mean?

Few questions can generate as many contradictory answers as what it means to be Latino or Hispanic. Part of the reason might be that it's hard to lump more than fifty million people—the U.S. Latino/Hispanic population according to the 2010 Census—from extremely different backgrounds into one neat classification. We Latinos come in different races, including white, black, Asian and Indian. We are Catholic and Jewish and Muslim. We gave birth to salsa, merengue, tango, samba, cumbia and reggeaton. Our food is eclectic, ancestral and full of flavor. We are passionate about our culture and proud of our heritage. We are immigrants and American citizens by birth. Some of us just got here; while others have always been here—after all, less than two hundred years ago, a large part of what is the United States today used to be part of Mexico. We can speak Spanish, English, and Spanglish. We are lawyers, janitors, doctors, journalists, stay-at-home moms and dads, politicians, construction workers, entrepreneurs, artists, bloggers, astronauts, farmers, and chefs. A homogeneous group we are not.

A BRIEF HISTORY OF LATINOS IN THE UNITED STATES

Immigration is intrinsically American. Without it, the United States would not exist. Period. I'm not interested in giving you a history lesson, but suffice it to say that unless you're Native American, there's no way you can deny that your ancestors were born in a country other than the United States of America and that they migrated to this side of the world in pursuit of some of the same ideals as current immigrants, namely, a better life for themselves and their families free of political, religious or economic persecution. To be clear, immigration has always been a contentious topic in this country, with the Italians, the Jews, the Irish and the Asians, among other groups, facing all kinds of racial and ethnic discrimination when they first arrived to the United States. And yet, the heated immigration debate currently overtaking this country seems to have taken the issue way too far with states like Arizona and Alabama passing draconian laws that practically make racial profiling legal. I don't think it would be too far-fetched to say that many Americans have forgotten where they came from and what their ancestors went through to get here. And while some may claim that this profiling has to do with the color of the skin of most Latinos or our supposed desire to get something for nothing, I think it has more to do with the fact that our immigration has been continuous and that full "assimilation" into the American culture hasn't been as successful as with prior immigrant groups.

But before I get into that, let's take an abbreviated look at this country's Hispanic immigration trends throughout history. Our history would be incomplete without talking about the many families in the Southwest who have lived on their lands since before they were a part of the United States as we know it today, something that many Americans don't seem to know (or don't care to remember). Brief history lesson: Prior to the Mexican-American War of 1846, Mexican territory included present-day California, Nevada, Utah, Arizona, New Mexico, Texas and parts of Colorado, Wyoming, Kansas and Oklahoma. When the Treaty of Guadalupe Hidalgo was signed signaling the end of the war in 1848, Mexico agreed to sell its northern territory to the United States and the new land owner agreed to extend U.S. citizenship to the Mexicans living in the transferred territory. Those who opted in, however, were always treated like second class citizens and weren't really ever considered American enough. This sentiment continued long after the Treaty was signed and new generations of Mexican-Americans felt the unequal treatment not that long ago. "They made us feel like we were foreigners, and we just wanted to feel like we were a part of the community," explained the Hon. Judge Roger Cisneros—one of the most notable Hispanics in Colorado—who was born in 1924 in New Mexico where he said he can trace his family's roots back more than four hundred years. In other words, way before the area became part of the United States. Like the popular saying invoked by many in similar a situation, "they didn't cross the border, rather the border crossed them."

The first real wave of immigrants who did cross the border between the United States and Mexico weren't treated any better. They came during and after both world wars mostly to provide cheap labor in areas decimated by the conflicts, such as farming. I think it's important to note that this type of immigration was encouraged by the United States itself through bilateral agreements like the Bracero Program (the Spanish word for day laborer), which brought temporary laborers from Mexico to work the fields, particularly in the

Southwest, at very low rates and with the assurance that they'd go back to Mexico once their work was done. Absolutely no strings attached. The lure of work for dirt-poor Mexicans coupled with the greed of farmers who loved the idea of getting their hands on cheap labor, opened up the door to illegal immigration. And so, just as many Mexican day laborers entered the country legally and temporarily, many also crossed the border illegally and never left (a trend that has obviously continued to this day). But, as they would find out soon enough, being a person of color in the United States at that time wasn't really a good thing. In many states, Mexicans (or anybody who spoke Spanish) were segregated just like blacks were in the South. In fact, it was not unusual to see signs with messages like "No Mexicans or dogs allowed" posted on the doors of establishments. In schools, kids were whipped if they spoke Spanish, and many parents were instructed to refrain from speaking to their children in their native tongue if they wanted to assimilate and become a part of their new culture and society. So the number one rule for many families was to never again utter a word of Spanish to their children, even if that meant they could barely communicate with them due to their own limited knowledge of English. Hence, for a whole generation of Latinos, Spanish became the language that would hold them back and be used to discriminate against them. That's how it came to slowly disappear, particularly in the southwestern part of the country.

"I don't remember being whipped, but we were put in classes for the 'educable mentally retarded' in the 1950s and 1960s only because we were Mexican and we spoke Spanish," said Luis Torres, the long time chairman of the Department of Chicano Studies at Metro State College of Denver and its current deputy provost. Torres grew up in a household where Spanish was predominant because his father was Mexican and, although he is bilingual, he didn't pass his Spanish on to his own children. "It's very hard to maintain your native language in a society which, in the past, has tried to keep people away from Spanish," Torres added.

Although some periods have been marked by higher migration from our neighboring country to the south, overall Mexican immigration has been a steady trend for decades. Lured by the possibility of better jobs and in the midst of the most gruesome and violent drug war of our times (with a death toll of 47,000 people since 2006 according to the Mexican government at the beginning of 2012), Mexicans have kept on coming to the United States. It's no surprise, then, that the largest Latino group in the United States—66% according to the 2010 Census—is of Mexican descent.

The second important immigration wave in the last hundred years took place in the 1940s and 1950s, and it involved Puerto Ricans. Even though some people don't see them as real immigrants since they are U.S. citizens by birth, the reality is that these people left their country, their culture and their language behind in exchange for better opportunities. Just like the Southwest looked to the Mexicans for help, the eastern side of the country was in need of cheap labor, and Puerto Ricans were desperate for jobs since the Great Depression and two world wars had left the island in dire financial straits. And while it's true that Puerto Ricans don't have to worry about any of the legal implications of other immigrants living and working in the United States, they were still victims of racial discrimination and have worked hard to put up a fight and let their voices be heard.

And heard they've been. As the second largest Hispanic group in the United States, Puerto Ricans have long enjoyed a strong presence in the military, educational, sports and political arenas. I mean, who can forget the momentous appointment of Sonia Sotomayor as the first Latina Supreme Court Justice in 2009? And, of course, it goes without saying that Puerto Ricans are the one Latino group that has dominated the arts and entertainment industry with talented artists who have become household names such as Jennifer Lopez, Marc Anthony, Ricky Martin, Rita Moreno, Jose Feliciano, Rosie Perez, Benicio del Toro, Dayanara Torres, Willie Colon, Hector Lavoe, Esmeralda Santiago… and the list goes on and on.

Today, there are Puerto Ricans all over the United States, but their historical concentration in New York and other northeastern states remains intact. I think it's fair to say that Puerto Ricans, more than any other Latino group in the United States, have been able to preserve their cultural heritage and the Spanish language, while assimilating into the American way of life. It's also fair to say that this might have a lot to do with the fact that, because they're American citizens, traveling back and forth between the island and the mainland is both easy and affordable, which means that they've been able to remain in constant contact with their language and culture.

Although this is not true at all of Cubans, the third largest Latino group in the country, they have also managed to keep their culture and *el español* alive—particularly in Miami, the city through which most Cubans enter the United States and where they pretty much rule. In their case, I'm inclined to say that power in numbers, as well as proximity to their homeland from which there is continuous migration, is what has allowed Cubans to keep their traditions and language alive. If you've had the privilege of visiting Miami, then you know that not speaking Spanish can be absolutely detrimental. I must say that landing in Miami was godsend when we moved to the United States from Peru. I seriously doubt that I would've been able to survive the culture (and language) shock if we had ended up in the heartland of America, for example.

Welcomed into the United States for political reasons —with two major waves of immigration in the 1960s and then in the 1980s— Cubans have also had a completely different experience than that of other immigrant groups because of their country's long standing communist regime. Cuban immigrants have what many consider a privileged situation as far as immigration is concerned. Thanks to the Cuban Adjustment Act they qualify for legal permanent residency status and eventually U.S. citizenship, as long as they make it to U.S. soil. This privileged position has been the source of contentious friction between Cuban immigrants and those of other nationalities who don't enjoy the same kind of benefits, even when their countries' governments are just as harsh or even more so.

Another major difference is that the first wave of immigrants out of Cuba after Fidel Castro took power were prosperous members of the middle class, including professionals, shop owners and businessmen. Without a doubt, their higher social status allowed for the political clout that Cuban-Americans hold today, particularly within the conservative ranks. Additionally, like Puerto Ricans, Cuban-Americans have also made huge strides in American culture, particularly in the areas of politics, sports and the arts.

And finally, there are the Central American immigrants, namely those from Nicaragua, El Salvador, Guatemala and Honduras—all countries ravaged by endless civil wars which took the lives of millions of innocent citizens whose family members had no choice but to flee in order to survive. Because it's estimated that more than two of every five Central Americans are here illegally, have low education levels and limited English proficiency, they face some of the toughest challenges in the United States as far as immigrant groups are concerned.

It should be clear, then, that taking into consideration our differences in country of origin, education, social status, race, Spanish and English language proficiency and immigrant experience, it is impossible to simply lump all Latinos together into just one category. And yet, how can we be counted otherwise? The issue of what to call ourselves has been debated to death and still we have no clear answer.

LATINO OR HISPANIC? WHICH IS IT?

Before moving from Peru to the United States as a teenager in 1987, the term Hispanic (*hispano*), which I rarely used, was a synonym for anything pertaining to the Iberian Peninsula (or Spain and Portugal). The term *latino* was used in reference to Latin, the classic language from which all romance languages, including Spanish, derive. Neither one of those terms were used to describe where I came from or what my heritage was. For the first fourteen years of my life, I was simply Peruvian. Little did I know that upon my arrival in Miami some would want me to lose that aspect of my identity and adopt the term Hispanic instead, even though I really didn't know exactly what that meant.

As I researched the topic for this book, however, I began to explore how these terms came to be and why so many people are adamant about what they like to be called.

Contrary to popular belief, the term Hispanic was not coined by Richard Nixon, but rather Grace Flores-Hughes, a Mexican-American who grew up in south Texas and worked as an assistant in the Department of Health, Education and Welfare. In the early 1970s Flores-Hughes was appointed to a committee to help choose the best name for the federal government to use when referring to people of mixed Spanish descent. In a 2009 interview with *The Washington Post,* Flores-Hughes said she pushed for the term Hispanic, which was included in all U.S. Census Bureau forms for the first time in 1980, because:

> "It best describes who we are based on our Hispanic surnames...The reason I am not in favor of "Latino" or "Latina" is that those terms can represent the people of the Mediterranean. Then you'd be including Portuguese and Italians, if you take it literally. And then it takes away from the Hispanic people of America that need to be counted..."

In the case of the term Latino, it's hard to pinpoint when it became popular among part of the population and why. Maybe the best explanation is that it's a short version of *latinoamericano*—the Spanish word for someone from Latin America—and for many, it better exemplifies their roots, which don't necessarily go back to Spain, as the term Hispanic can suggest. Interestingly enough, Latin American seems to have been the preferred term for many activists in the 1960s and 1970s as is evident in their choice of names for the nonprofit organizations they founded during that time: LULAC (League of United Latin American Citizens), LAEF (Latin American Educational Foundation) and LAYC (Latin American Youth Center), to name a few.

So which term is the correct one? That question is impossible to answer because, fundamentally, it depends on a person's preference. Today, many people who would be considered Hispanic continue to have issues using that term to identify themselves and prefer to be called Latino instead. This is especially true for the younger generation and those who live in the western part of the country. Some have gone as far as saying that Hispanic is the preferred label of the conservatives while liberals would rather use Latino. Although both terms ultimately mean the same thing and refer to the same group of people, they're not without their differences. One of the most obvious ones is that Hispanic is an English word whereas Latino/a is a Spanish word used in English. From what I've been able to gather, two points stand out more than others in the debate for those who take issue with the term Hispanic. The first one is that they feel like Hispanic is a term imposed by the government to classify a minority group. In other words, the name was chosen by the powers that be—even though it was a Mexican-American who coined the term—and not by the people.

Well known Chicana author Sandra Cisneros has been very open about her dislike of the term Hispanic, going as far as refusing to be photographed for the cover of *Hispanic Magazine* in which in 2000 she was quoted as saying: "The term Hispanic makes my skin crawl. It's a very colonistic term, a disrespectful term, a term imposed on us without asking what we wanted to call ourselves."

Which brings us to second issue that many have with term, which is that the definition of Hispanic is directly related to Spain or Spanish-speaking countries. For many Latinos, especially those with direct ties to Latin America, this only conjures up memories of the atrocities committed by the Spanish conquistadors in the countries they colonized. Many in Latin America feel that Spain will always be responsible for their country's woes because of the systematic abuse and oppression they perpetrated on the natives in the name of *La Conquista*. Furthermore, those who prefer the term Latino claim that Hispanic makes reference to a country they have no ties to, for they consider themselves more indigenous or black than white European. But this distinction is exactly why lots of other people prefer the term Hispanic, especially those of Mexican-American ancestry in the southwestern of the United States. Many of these families have lived in those areas since time immemorial—when the states they now live in were part of first Spain and then Mexico prior to the Treaty of Guadalupe Hidalgo in 1848—and can trace their roots all the way back to Spain, something of which they are very proud.

Either way, Hispanic continues to be the preferred term of the two, according to the results of a 2012 survey titled "When Labels Don't Fit: Hispanics and Their Views of Identity" by the Pew Hispanic Center, which found that 33% of respondents prefer the term Hispanic, while 14% feel Latino describes them best. Fifty-one percent however, said they had no preference and that might have a lot to do with how most Latinos (51%) prefer to use their actual country of origin (or that of their parents) to describe themselves. That's definitely true of myself. I don't really like either term, but when pressed to choose one I'd rather go with Latina. My personal preference, though, has really nothing to do with the issues discussed here, but is more based on the fact that if it's short for *latinoamericana*, it definitely describes me better than Hispanic. Yet, more often than not, I simply call myself Peruvian because that's what I am.

Although my children are still too little, I've already started thinking about how they will see themselves and which term they'll prefer because, again, our circumstances are completely different. Like many Hispanic children today, while my husband and I share the same heritage, we were born in different countries and thus we bring different cultural traditions to the table. I find it very difficult to believe that my children will feel either Peruvian or Puerto Rican, but it somehow seems more likely that they'll better identify with the term Latino. I guess time will tell.

While it doesn't seem likely that this debate will be settled any time soon, it's interesting to see the latest tendency of some of the major news outlets, for example, in naming the content they've created geared toward Latinos: FoxNewsLatino, NBC Latino, AOL Latino and Huffington Post's Latino Voices. Notice the absence of the term Hispanic. Meanwhile, the tendency within the mainstream media and in many organizations and companies is to use the terms interchangeably so as to be more inclusive, as we've done in this book.

ANA SPEAKS OUT ON THE RISE OF LATINOS

I AM ONE OF THOSE LATINAS WHO HAS NEVER FELT IDENTIFIED WITH THE TERM Hispanic, for all of the reasons Roxana mentions. To me Hispanic has always felt antiquated, corporate and stale. Not only that, it denies my identity as a *mujer Latina*. The term is genderless and goes against one of the main distinctions of the Spanish language to give a male or female personality to most objects. So, being called Hispanic groups me into an all male and female category of people from Latin America and Spain. No, I am not Hispanic, *soy Latina*, and a very proud one at that.

I started realizing I was, indeed, Latina when I went to college, first at the University of Texas in Austin and then at the University of Florida. Since I had just come back from living my formative years in El Salvador, I naturally gravitated to any circle of Spanish speakers and Latinos I could find. Together, we created our mini subculture of gatherings featuring our local foods, parties full of salsa, merengue and Latin rock music, as well as a support system for all of us who were living so far away from our families. This was back in the early 1990's when Latinos and our culture were still not mainstream.

I graduated in 1996 with a Bachelor of Arts in TV & Radio Production. I was lucky enough to have a couple of options as to where to start my career, but I was focused on one place only: Univision in Miami. To put things into perspective, this was way before Univision was competing in the same field with the four national networks. This was when Sofía Vergara was hosting a show called *Fuera de Serie* and Hollywood seemed miles away. This was also when Selena had just risen to stardome and then disappeared, leaving a huge gap for those young Latinas who lost their first icon. When Shakira was played on CDs our friends from Latin America would send to us because it was the hot thing over there. Yet, Miami and Univision is where I felt connected at that stage of my life and part of me knew it was the epicenter of huge things to come for all Latinos.

I can clearly remember the day when Ricky Martin got up on stage at the Grammys to sing *Living la Vida Loca*, when he put our culture's energy on a pedestal for all to see. My friend and I were at a bar in South Beach and we both got chills because we just knew this was the beginning of something big. Latinos were on their way to becoming mainstream. With that, of course, would come bigger and better opportunities for all of us in the entertainment business and otherwise.

Fifteen years later, I am still very involved with the Latino entertainment world, but now with many more options and a vibrant playing field. The world of blogs and social media has created an open space for Latinas and Latinos to clearly make their voice and their presence known. As a group, we have been slower to adopt the new technologies, but now we are certainly leaving our mark. Groups like Latinos in Social Media (LATISM) and Voto Latino have been able to quickly gather masses of online Latinos to rally and collaborate around important social and political causes, giving the new face of America a platform of expression.

Another group which has become a force to be reckoned with are Latina bloggers. Through my other enterprise, Latina Bloggers Connect, Inc, we've been able to create a network of bloggers who self-identify as Latinas and who are creating content which speaks to our community in both English and Spanish. These women are moms, students, fashionistas, doctors, teachers, artists, entrepreneurs, etc who feel the need to go online to share their voices and experiences and thus continue to shine a light on our experience as Latinas in the United States.

I've called myself Latina for a little over two decades now, and I can clearly say it's been exciting to witness how the melding of cultures is taking Latino culture to the forefront of mainstream America.

THE NEW FACE OF AMERICA

So what, then, does it really mean to be Latino/Hispanic in the United States today? For the majority of us both terms ultimately carry connotations of pride in our family, our roots and our heritage, but there really isn't a right or wrong answer to this question. We are a diverse group with similar but different traditions, music and food. The immigrant experience of the Cuban-American is nothing like that of the Mexican-American. Yet, for all our marked differences, the one thing we all share—albeit in different levels of fluency—is a native tongue. While there is a large group of Latinos who don't speak Spanish, most of us do. Even those who don't speak Spanish understand a few words here and there because it's part of our heritage.

In fact, thirty seven million people ages five and older speak Spanish at home (and more than half of those people, 55.3%, also speak English "very well"), according to the 2010 American Community Survey, an ongoing yearly study by the U.S. Census Bureau. Spanish, then, is the second most used language in the United States, especially in states like California, Texas, Arizona, New Mexico and Florida, where the majority of the Latino population resides.

Having lived in Miami for most of my life in the United States (before moving to Denver in 2006), I know firsthand that not speaking Spanish can be detrimental because the truth is you can't escape it. You hear it in supermarkets, restaurants, parks, malls, schools, television and radio stations and in government offices. One of the biggest reasons why the culture shock was minimal when I first arrived there as a teenager was that, even back in the late 1980s, Miami felt like an extension of Latin America. In fact, the running joke has always been that the best thing about Miami is that it's so close to the United States! In other words, Miami is heaven for those of us who are trying to raise bilingual and bicultural children because the exposure to both our native language and culture happens organically. I imagine it's the same in cities like Los Angeles, Houston, Chicago and New York.

Looking back, I realize how much I took for granted the fact that I lived and breathed the Latino culture every day and everywhere for the first nineteen years of my life in this country. My husband and I often joke that when we moved to Denver it felt like we had finally arrived to the United States. Not that there aren't any Latinos here—we make up one fifth of Colorado's population—but we're more dispersed. And, unless you visit specific pockets within the city, Spanish is not prevalent here, especially if you live in the suburbs. Raising bilingual children, then, becomes a challenge.

Luckily, this might not be the case for long.

LATINOS ARE AS AMERICAN AS APPLE PIE

All across the United States, things are changing. For starters, Latinos were the fastest growing segment of the population between 2000 and 2010, according to the U.S. Census Bureau, with a whopping 43% increase. States that have traditionally had smaller Latino populations—like South Carolina, Alabama, Tennessee, Kentucky and Arkansas—showed an unprecedented jump as Latinos moved there in search of better opportunities. In other words, it's getting harder and harder to move around the country without bumping into a Latino community somewhere. The U.S. Census Bureau estimates that the Latino population will soar to nearly 133 million people by 2050.

And even though the anti-immigrant backlash is as alive as it has ever been, our sheer numbers have allowed us to wield our power as a collective group in more than one area.

Politics: It's no secret that Latinos will most likely end up deciding the November 2012 presidential elections, particularly in the key battleground states of Florida, Arizona, Nevada and Colorado. Most political pundits agree that whoever takes the majority of Latino votes will win the White House. In fact, this is such an important topic that *Time* magazine not only considered it worthy of its cover earlier this year (March 5, 2012 issue), but it also wrote the main headline entirely in Spanish: *Yo Decido*. To explain, it included the following sub-headline in English: Why Latinos will Pick the Next President.

Furthermore, earlier this year, the Democratic party—aware of the power of Latinos and in an effort to make sure we get on their side—named Los Angeles Mayor Antonio Villaraigosa chairman of the Democratic National Convention. Although Villaraigosa hasn't spoken explicitly about his own political plans, many see the third Mexican-American to hold the mayoral post in the second largest city in the country as a force to be reckoned with.

Of course, he's not the only Latino in a position of power in the political/governmental arena. Others include Sonia Sotomayor, the first Latina Supreme Court Associate Justice, the current Secretary of the Interior Ken Salazar, the current Secretary of Labor Hilda Solis and Susana Martinez, the first Latina governor.

Economy: According to an April 2012 Nielsen report, the U.S. Hispanic community is among the world's top 20 economies. With over 50 million Latinos currently spending about $1 trillion a year, the report states that our buying power will increase 50% to $1.5 trillion by 2015. Essentially, the future success of the U.S. economy will rely heavily on Latinos and how we spend our money. The most interesting part of the report — at least for me — was the finding that "Hispanics are the largest immigrant group to exhibit significant culture sustainability and are not disappearing into the American melting pot." This only goes to show the importance we place on our Latino heritage, but also our refusal to just blend into one of our two cultures.

Language: Spanish, the second most spoken language in the United States—the largest Spanish-speaking country in the world after Mexico—has been leaving its mark on mainstream American culture for a long time. From the highly despised by many nativists "Press 1 for English and 2 for Spanish," to bilingual signs and government forms (including the highly contested bilingual ballots), Spanish is hard to escape in major Latino hubs across the country. In cities like Miami it's not unusual to find that the majority of those working in customer service are usually bilingual. But Spanish has found its way into this country's vernacular even in areas where Hispanic presence is not as widespread. Take, for example, words like taco, macho, burrito, fiesta, amigo, cilantro, poncho, barrio, piñata, siesta, coyote, hombre, cojones, tortilla, rodeo, salsa, cabana, guerrilla, loco, sombrero, patio—all of Spanish origin but today considered part of the English language (you can find them all in the dictionary).

Not one to ever lag behind, the media has also jumped on the Spanish bandwagon. It's not unusual to hear my native tongue on hit TV shows like ABC's hugely popular sitcom *Modern Family* with Colombian actress Sofia Vergara, *Ugly*

Betty and episodes of *The Good Wife* with Honduran-American actress America Ferrara and on the network's short-lived medical drama *Off the Map*, which was supposed to take place in a remote South American village. Other network shows, such as CBS's *CSI: Miami*, justify the use of Spanish by saying it makes their characters more authentic. And who can forget Dora the Explorer? Although she's not my favorite character in the world—I find her voice just a tad annoying—Nickelodeon's Dora has done wonders in terms of making bilingualism cool in the eyes of children!

Food: I don't think anyone can deny that no other aspect of Latino culture has made its way into mainstream America like our food. From fast food chains like Taco Bell, Qdoba and Chipotle to top rated Mexican restaurants all over the country, including celebrity chef Rick Bayless' highly-awarded eateries in Chicago. I've traveled my fair share within the United States and I have yet to visit one single place, regardless of its size, where there are no Mexican or Tex-Mex restaurants. Mexican fare, like nachos and quesadillas, is the norm in lots of so-called American restaurants as are alcoholic beverages such as margaritas, Mexican beer and tequila. In cities with large Mexican populations, it's not unusual to find mainstream supermarkets selling Mexican products like tortillas, Mexican hot chocolate and refried beans. Nor is it uncommon for many of these cities to have their own markets solely dedicated to the sale of Mexican products.

Even though Mexican food is the most widely known, cuisines from other Latin American countries, including my own, are starting to become more well known among a more open America, full of people ready to try new flavors. In September 2011, the ambassador of Peruvian cuisine, renown chef Gaston Acurio, opened up his second restaurant in the United

States on none other than Madison Avenue in New York City (the first one is at the famed Embarcadero in San Francisco).

Latin music: From salsa to reggaeton and everything in between, who doesn't want to learn to dance to the beats of Latin music? Salsa is probably the most popular genre among the American crowd with scores of dance studios and night clubs offering lessons in a growing number of cities across the country thanks, in large part, to salsa legends like the great Celia Cruz and current popular stars like Marc Anthony. But thanks to hugely successful cross-over artists like Shakira, Ricky Martin and Enrique Iglesias, to name a few, and bilingual stars like Pitbull, other Latino musical genres are also becoming more mainstream.

A NEW BILINGUAL PARENTING REVOLUTION

So what does all this mean in terms of the usage and popularity of Spanish in this country? With nearly one in every three Americans being Latino in the not so distant future, I think it's safe to assume that Spanish is not going anywhere. While it'll probably continue to be inexplicably and absurdly tied to the immigration debate, Spanish can only continue to permeate all aspects of our daily lives and hopefully gain some deserved respect as the number of Latinos in this country continues to increase.

It should be noted that while studies have shown that an immigrant's native language is all but dead by the third generation—and that has certainly been the case in many areas throughout the Southwest—I believe that this is unlikely to happen to Spanish because of the constant influx of new immigration from Spanish-speaking countries. Furthermore, as we've seen from many of our Latino readers, who for whatever reasons were not raised to be bilingual, once they become parents there's a huge need for them to reconnect to their heritage by making sure their children learn Spanish. This change of mentality has sparked what we like to refer to as the bilingual parenting revolution.

Take the story of Kayla Rodriguez, a mom of two who was born in Florida to Cuban-American parents. Her father was in the military so she spent most of her life in the United Kingdom. Rodriguez said her mom spoke to her and her siblings in Spanish when they were younger and closer to the rest of their Latino family, but things changed once they moved to England. "The only time my mother would say something in Spanish was when we got in trouble for something, but we would never hear it after that," Rodriguez explained. "All of my parents' friends spoke English so there was really no reason for them to speak Spanish, from what they say."

Rodriguez's husband, whose family is from Puerto Rico, has a similar story. He wasn't raised to be bilingual either because his parents wanted him to learn English—the story of so many immigrants who mistakenly think that Spanish must be forgotten in order to learn English and assimilate. The couple has been intent on relearning Spanish through online courses, books and magazines. "I regret not being bilingual everyday. I have a lot of Latino friends that know Spanish fluently, and they just talk away, and my husband and I just stand there speaking as much as we can and trying to pick everything up," Rodriguez said. "We always look at each other and say, 'I cannot believe our parents did not teach us Spanish'. It just really makes us feel low some times."

Wanting to prevent their own children from feeling like that, the couple knew—even before they became parents—that they would raise their children to be bilingual. "I did not want my children to be in the same situation that I was in, not knowing how to speak Spanish, and then growing up and asking me the same questions I asked my parents, mainly my mother," Rodriguez added. But they're also raising their kids to be bilingual for the same reasons most Latinos are doing so. "Since Spanish is part of my children's culture, I think it is very important that they know it. It's an important part of their heritage," she said. Rodriguez is only one of many Latino parents who didn't necessarily grow up bilingual themselves, but who are now helping plant the seeds for our native language to endure for generations to come.

But Latinos are not the only ones leading this bilingual parenting revolution. In fact, for a large chunk of our blog's readers, Spanish is in no way, shape or form part of their heritage, yet they've chosen to raise their children to be bilingual. There are many reasons why non-Latino parents would want this for their children, and for a lot of them the love affair with Spanish and all things Latino starts way before they even have children. "My interest in Spanish took off in college. I took a Spanish class, and one of my college roommates was from Puerto Rico. [We] became very close friends, and I became immersed in Spanish via our friendship," reminisced Susan O. Stephan, one of our blog's regular contributors and a mom of two boys she's raising to be trilingual. "She would take me to parties where everyone was speaking Spanish and even took me to Puerto Rico with her during Spring Break."

Amy Conroy, an occasional contributor to SpanglishBaby who's raising three bilingual children by dividing their time between their home in Los Angeles and their adopted home in Mexico, has a similar story. "I was first introduced to Spanish as a Freshman in high school and emerged four years later with little more than, '*Hola, chica!*'. I longed to travel, so I studied a semester abroad in Salamanca, Spain, while I was at UCLA. Again, the term 'study' should be used lightly here, though I did fall in love with the culture and language. I later pursued a Master's in Anthropology, which afforded me the opportunity to live and study in Central America."

Once both women became moms, they knew they wanted to raise their children to be bilingual, even though Spanish is not their native tongue.

"I was originally concerned that I would be hurting my children's cognitive development by speaking to them only in Spanish since it is not my native language. I did a considerable amount of research prior to their births and found that the cognitive benefits from being bilingual would actually be beneficial to my children," said Stephan whose boys are spoken to in Spanish by mom, in German by dad and in English by everyone else.

Both moms said they're well aware of not only the cognitive benefits of being bilingual, but also the cultural ones in terms of how much broader their children's world is and their exposure to other ways of living. And while they agreed that speaking any second language accomplishes this, they are both well aware of the weight Spanish has and will continue to have in the United States in the years to come. "For me, living in California, Spanish has always been practical and useful, and therefore has remained an active and vital part of my life," said Conroy, who spent part of 2011 and part of 2012 in San Miguel de Allende, Mexico, immersing her children and herself in the culture of their second language.

Stephan, who also lives in California, had this to say about her decision to teach her children Spanish:

"It is not essential that a child's second language be Spanish, but it is certainly useful in the United States. My children are also learning German. They speak it with their father, but unfortunately they have very few opportunities to speak German with others. They use Spanish all the time. Almost every time we go to the park, they find a friend who can speak Spanish too. It is nice to teach children a language that they actually can use."

Some people fall so hard for the Latino culture and the Spanish language that they end up marrying into it. Such was the case for Chelsea Kyle, who married a Latino with whom she has a three-year-old son. Although they're no longer together, Kyle—who is a Spanish tutor—has made it a point to make sure their son grows up speaking Spanish and is surrounded by his Latino heritage, which luckily for them is not hard to do in their native Orlando, Florida. "Even if my son did not have Puerto Rican and Cuban roots on his father's side, I would speak Spanish to him. I don't just consider Spanish an advantage in personal and business life; I consider it a necessity, given the rapidly increasing Latino population of the United States," Kyle explained, adding that a child who grows up with more than one language "has a built-in sense of tolerance, an innate open heart." And who could argue with that?

But what about those parents who have no cultural connection to Hispanics and *no hablan* an iota of Spanish and yet they are doing everything they can to make sure their children grow up speaking the language? After understanding the amazing benefits of raising bilingual children, Sarah Auerswald decided to enroll her children in a popular dual language Spanish immersion program in Los Angeles, even though neither she nor her husband speak the language. In fact, Auerswald, who was born in New York and grew up in Hawaii, said that she studied Spanish in high school—like

many Americans are required to do in order to graduate—
but didn't really learn a thing, as she can't speak it today.
And so, after doing some research about second language
acquisition and finding out that the younger children start
to learn a new language the better, she knew she couldn't
pass up the opportunity to have her children attend the dual
language program by her house coveted by so many parents.

"I knew I wanted my kids to be immersed in Spanish so
that they would become fluent because I knew it would be so
important for them to be able to speak [it] growing up in the
21st Century and in Los Angeles," Auerswald shared.

Besides knowing that learning a second language comes
much more naturally to children, Auerswald also appreciates
the other benefits of growing up bilingual and doesn't understand why it isn't the norm in the United States. "I know people
who grew up in Europe, Asia or South America who speak multiple languages and I am always so impressed with them. Being able to communicate in many languages is such an asset,"
said Auerswald. "And especially here in Los Angeles, there are
so many people around us who speak Spanish it would be so
smart to be able to freely communicate with them all—and I
really wanted that for my kids. I would hope that their language learning does not stop with Spanish. My hope is for them
to take a third language in high school. And after that, who
knows?"

Like many parents in her situation, Auerswald is living proof
that you can still raise bilingual children even if you are monolingual yourself. It's definitely not easy, and Auerswald doesn't
claim otherwise, but if you really want this for your children,
it's absolutely doable. Auerswald said she relies on the help of
other bilingual parents whenever she needs a translation and
she works in conjunction with her sons' teachers to make sure

they have all the necessary resources to support their second language. This community aspect of dual language programs, where everyone is involved in the language learning process, is one of my favorite parts of this type of bilingual education. It's as if the only way for a program like this to survive is by ensuring that everyone is involved and working as a team. But we'll delve into the beauty behind bilingual education a bit later.

In the meantime, I hope I've been successful at painting a picture of a new United States, which shows that, whether some people like it or not, Latinos are here to stay and are as much a part of the American fabric as any other ethnic group. I can only hope that by the time my kids become adults, we can all come to the agreement that while being Latino means having ties to a rich cultural legacy from south of the border, it also means having a deep connection to the United States, its traditions, customs and languages. No one should have to choose one language and culture over the other because having both is undeniably better than having just one, and I'm a prime example of that. As a fully bilingual (and bicultural) woman, I'm totally convinced that my two languages have made my life much richer than it would've been had I spoken only Spanish or only English. I'm pretty sure Ana feels the same way. Knowing first hand that being bilingual is better, it's only logical for us to want to share this truly amazing way of raising children with as many parents as possible.

Why Bilingual Is Better

ANA L. FLORES

BEFORE I GOT PREGNANT WITH MY ONE-AND-ONLY GIRL, I NEVER gave the concept of "raising a bilingual child" much thought. All I knew was that my husband and I both spoke Spanish to each other and as a first choice among friends, and that we would naturally speak Spanish to our daughter. But not with a laid-out plan or a specific method because, well, that's just so not our style! I guess we naively thought the Spanish-fluency gene would automatically be passed on to her at birth, just like my curls and her dad's blonde looks would be.

But once she was born and we delved into an almost helicopter parenting mode, we began to ask ourselves some of the same questions many families ask themselves about raising bilingual children. Would hearing more than one language from birth be confusing for a child's seemingly small, undeveloped brain? Would it put her at a cognitive and social disadvantage? Is there even any real benefit whatsoever to make it worth the hard work of raising a bilingual child? We knew in our hearts that raising our daughter in two languages would be good for her, but was there any solid evidence to back that up? That's when the parenting books, websites and blogs came in, not that we found a whole lot of information out there for bilingual families at that time.

While we truly believe that bilingual is better, in the United States we are fighting against decades of solid belief systems based on ignorance, social oppression, xenophobia and a false assumption that assimilation means completely letting go of your heritage language and customs in order to become fully American. There are so many misconceptions about growing up multilingual that have been continuously perpetuated from one generation to the next, but thankfully there is also a great deal of scientific evidence which can help us separate fact from fiction.

Before we start exploring the many advantages of being raised in more than one language, let's take a look at five of the most common myths about raising bilingual children. Hopefully this valuable information will be enough to debunk some of the major myths associated with bilingualism, once and for all.

COMMON MYTHS
ABOUT RAISING BILINGUAL CHILDREN

• Growing up with two or more languages will only confuse your child.

According to everything we've read, this misconception has been around for a long time and apparently it goes back to immigration issues in the United States. Educators used to tell immigrant parents that it was better for their children to speak English at home, erroneously stating that early exposure to two languages put children at a disadvantage. This is why there are so many third generation Chavez(es) or Rodriguez(es) in the west who do not speak a word of Spanish. Newer research, however, actually shows there are many advantages to being bilingual,which we'll be exploring in detail later on.

From my personal observations, my daughter Camila never experienced any confusion at all. She has always known who to speak to in Spanish and who to speak to in English and will automatically make the switch.

We have a very good friend, Dariela Cruz, who is Venezuelan and married to a man from the United States. She only speaks Spanish to her two kids and her husband speaks to them in English. My daughter and her son have been friends ever since they were about two years old and have seen each other frequently. Of course, when Dariela and I get together for playdates, Spanish is the name of the game. As the kids grew, her son started refusing to speak in Spanish even to her and opted for English. However, we were always amazed that as soon as he saw Camila and me, he would speak to us *en español* because it seemed as though he thought I wouldn't understand otherwise! He clearly was not confused, he was just going through a typical phase of rebellion against the minority language.

- It takes longer for bilingual children to learn how to speak.

The author of *Raising a Bilingual Child,* Barbara Zurer Pearson, says this myth is not supported by any scientific evidence. In fact, "with respect to most developmental language milestones, bilinguals are either at the same level as or ahead of monolinguals." Additionally, bilinguals have been found to have greater cognitive flexibility in word learning than monolinguals. Bilinguals were able to learn words with similar meanings more readily than monolinguals.

Both my daughter and Roxana's two children were exposed to both languages in-utero, with a heavier influence of

Spanish, and none of them experienced a delay in learning to speak. Camila, my girl, did have a problem with the clarity of her speech, but that would have happened if she only knew one language as well. Though some children may know more words in one language than in the other, it's the total number of words acquired in both languages that matters when it comes to speech development milestones.

If you do suspect a delay in your budding bilingual's speech, make sure you get him assessed by a speech therapist who speaks his language and who has experience dealing with children who know multiple languages. Be very wary of any doctor or teacher who tells you to stop speaking a second language to your child.

- They will only end up mixing both languages and won't know either well.

Mixing languages is inevitable and it's harmless. But to many monolinguals, it's proof that a child isn't really able to tell his languages apart. The actual term for this behavior is "code-switching" and there's absolutely nothing wrong with it. Code-switching is used for a number of reasons but does not necessarily indicate a language deficit. Sometimes bilinguals code-switch for emphasis or to express a term that has a slightly different meaning.

In some regions code-switching is the norm. It is important to consider a child's language model. If children grow up in a code-switching region, they will likely code-switch. What is important to determine is whether or not they are able to use the languages separately after being sufficiently exposed to non code-switching models.

Personally, I code-switch and it's not because I'm not *completely* fluent in both English and Spanish, but because sometimes a word sounds better in the language I'm not using. In fact, I have been quoted several times saying I'm most comfortable when I'm speaking with another Spanish/English bilinguals because my brain can relax and switch back and forth to whichever language works best for what I'm trying to say. This was definitely one of the bonding factors for my friendship with Roxana!

- It's too late.

It is *never* too late. It is only easier when children are younger. We always get asked if there's a window of opportunity for the ideal age to raise bilingual kids. There are actually several windows, or critical periods, for language learning when our brain is most adaptive to absorbing new language(s), the broadest being from birth to seven years of age, even before we learn to talk.

The Bilingual Baby Project—a fascinating study we'll be taking a closer look at later on—has concluded that the earlier we start exposing babies to a second language, the more flexible their bilingual brains will be and the more they will be able to identify and separate the sounds of the different languages they are exposed to.

However, with the right consistency and exposure, a child can adapt to a second language even after this first window of opportunity has closed. It would just be less organic and more of a process, but Roxana herself is proof *que ¡sí se puede!*

• Children with language impairment should not learn more than one language at a time.

There is no evidence that being raised with two languages will confuse children with normal language development or children with language impairment. A recent study found that children with language impairment who came from bilingual backgrounds did not have more severe language problems than monolinguals with language impairment.

Now that we've debunked the old myths about raising bilinguals, let's explore together the many amazing reasons why bilingual truly is better.

BILINGUALISM IS BETTER FOR YOUR BRAIN

In the last couple of years an overwhelming amount of research has come out praising the advantages of the bilingual brain. Benefits ranging from an increase in multitasking abilities to a delay in the onset of Alzheimer's disease among bilinguals are quickly making people realize that being monolingual is like having two hands and being taught how to use only one. We are born with the innate ability to learn more than one language, yet we, as a culture, prefer to ignore such amazing brain capacity because we just don't understand how to make it happen or we're too afraid to go against the monolingual mainstream norm.

Researchers in the areas of neuroscience, linguistics and psychology all over the world have been conducting fascinating studies on bilingualism using the latest neuroimaging technologies, among other methods. The beauty of neuroimaging is that it essentially lets us peek into the functioning process of the information centers of the brain. Imagine that? We can now see into a bilingual's brain and clearly map out how extraordinary it is and how it differs, in many ways, from a monolingual brain.

Neuroimaging and other types of methodologies are proving that our kids are excellent multitaskers, they can concentrate better, their brains are more flexible, they are better readers and they even have an edge over Alzheimer's disease. Sounds outrageous? Well, we've got proof.

Your Baby is a Language Learning Machine

One of the most remarkable things about all the studies involving bilinguals is that they prove just how amazing the human brain truly is. According to a 2009 study, "babies being raised bilingual—by simply speaking to them in two languages—can learn both in the time it takes most babies to learn one." The main reason has to do with our brain's flexibility and how exposure to two languages from early on makes the brain even more flexible.

For this study, conducted by scientists at Italy's International School for Advanced Studies and published in the journal *Science,* researchers tested more than forty twelve-month-old bilingual and monolingual babies. Researchers concluded that the bilingual babies who participated in the study were capable of learning two kinds of sound patterns at the same time while the monolingual babies learned just one.

A 2010 study published in *Psychological Science* also found that babies are perfectly fit to learn more than two languages and distinguish between them, but also found that mothers play a huge role in early bilingualism. Researchers from the University of British Columbia concluded that "hearing two languages regularly during pregnancy puts infants on the road to bilingualism by birth." If the mother is regularly speaking two languages to her unborn baby, or even if she is speaking one language and the father is speaking another one consistently, this bilingual exposure can affect the newborn's language preferences. Just as a child is able to recognize his mother's voice as soon as he leaves the womb, he also demonstrates the ability to listen to and pay attention to those languages he heard consistently while in the womb.

The Bilingual Baby Project is another study conducted by researchers from the University of Washington and the University of Texas at San Antonio, which recruited thirty children to document the development of their brains and their language acquisition in a bilingual environment over a span of five years. What is unique about this project is how it brought together sociologists, neuroscientists and educators to use testing methods from a wide range of scientific and sociological areas.

This multi-year study concluded that the earlier we start exposing babies to a second language, the more flexible their bilingual brains will be and the more they can identify and separate the sounds of the different languages they are exposed to. Another interesting finding from this study also involves the important role of parents in the process of raising bilingual children. Researchers pointed out that "the amount of exposure to each language, the strategies the babies' parents used to promote bilingualism in their homes and parents' desires to raise bilingual children were very important in their babies' bilingual comprehension."

As you can see from these studies, babies' brains are programmed to learn multiple languages, but they need us—parents—to fuel this capacity and turn on the switch.

Bilingual Children Concentrate Better

Another recent study by researchers at Cornell Language Acquisition Lab concluded that bilingual children are able to concentrate better than their monolingual counterparts. According to the scientists, "children who learn a second language can maintain attention despite outside stimuli better than children who know only one language." This ability to concentrate better can positively contribute to a child's future academic success, the study went on to explain. This study sheds light on the clear cognitive advantage for bilingual children as they develop an ability to focus on achieving goals, further giving them a competitive edge where education is concerned.

In other words, "Cognitive advantages follow from becoming bilingual," says Barbara Lust, a developmental psychologist and linguistics expert, as well as one of the researchers for this study. "These cognitive advantages can contribute to a child's future academic success."

The academic edge attributed to the bilingual brain is further documented in a study conducted by a team of researchers from Concordia University and York University in Canada and the Université de Provence in France. As reported in the *Journal of Experimental Child Psychology*, "the research team tested the understanding of English and French words among twenty-four-month-olds to see if bilingual toddlers had acquired comparable vocabulary in each language."

71

A series of tests were conducted among sixty-three mono-lingual and native bilingual toddlers to examine whether bi-lingual children this young would also demonstrate the ability to outperform monolingual kids on tasks measuring executive functioning skills. What the researchers found is that bilin-guals outperformed monolinguals on tasks during which they were distracted. This is attributed to "bilinguals' extensive practice in exercising selective attention and cognitive flex-ibility during language use because both languages are active when one of them is being used." Basically meaning that since both languages are active in a bilingual's brain at all times, bi-linguals must constantly be choosing which language, word or phrase to use at any given moment. Since bilingual children start developing this executive function in the brain as soon as they are immersed in multiple languages, over time they become more efficient at it, making them better prepared to sort out what's important at any particular moment.

Dr. Ellen Bialystok, a renowned cognitive neuroscientist, has spent four decades examining the many benefits of bilin-gualism for the mind. In a recent 2011 study, conducted for York University in Canada, she tested the coordination of ex-ecutive function in monolingual and bilingual children. In an interview for *The New York Times,* Bialystok described how the bilingual children in the study outshined the monolin-guals: "As we did our research, you could see there was a big difference in the way monolingual and bilingual children pro-cessed language. We found that if you gave five and six-year-olds language problems to solve, monolingual and bilingual children knew, pretty much, the same amount of language. But on one question, there was a difference. We asked all the children if a certain illogical sentence was grammatically correct: 'Apples grow on noses.' The monolingual children couldn't answer. They'd say, 'That's silly' and they'd stall. But the bilingual children would say, in their own words, 'It's silly, but it's grammatically correct.' The bilinguals, we found, manifested a cognitive system with the ability to attend to important information and ignore the less important."

More is clearly more when it comes to a bilingual brain. Instead of multiple languages being confusing to a child, the more they are richly immersed in two or more languages from an early age, the more their brains reach their full capabilities.

Bilingualism Improves Reading Speed and Comprehension

According to a fascinating 2009 study which was published in *Psychological Science*, bilingual individuals are unable to "switch off" a language completely, meaning that a second language is always present in the thought processes of bilingual individuals. Researchers studied this phenomenon in forty-five university students whose native language was Dutch and secondary language was English. The subjects were asked to read several sentences containing both cognates (words that have a similar meaning and form across several languages, such as "leopard" and "leopardo" in English and Spanish) and control words. The study clearly revealed that readers spent less time processing the cognates than the control words as they read, suggesting that the knowledge of words with similar meanings in both languages actually reinforces reading skills and comprehension in the native language.

Of course the implications of this particular study vary according to the language combinations spoken in each bilingual family (there are obviously more English/Spanish or Spanish/French cognates than Japanese/Swedish ones), but this is very encouraging, as it highlights just one more reason why giving our children the gift of bilingualism is so important.

A more recent 2011 study by researchers from York University in Toronto also revealed that bilingual children have a deeper understanding of the structure of language itself, thus gaining benefits in literacy skills over monolinguals. It may take some bilingual children a bit longer to pick up both languages, but that only means they are processing much more information which will later prove to be beneficial to their overall cognitive development.

What parent wouldn't want to provide her children with that possibility?

Being Bilingual Makes it Easier to Learn New Languages

As if all these were not reasons enough to raise bilingual children, the researchers behind a 2009 Northwestern University study published in *Psychonomic Bulletin and Review* tested the ability of sixty university students (twenty monolinguals, twenty early English-Mandarin speakers and twenty early English-Spanish speakers) in their early twenties to learn new languages, controlling for age, education, English language vocabulary size and, in the case of bilinguals, second language proficiency.

What they found is that it's easier for bilinguals than for monolinguals to learn a new foreign language, and, again, that the earlier children are exposed to a second language, the greater the benefits. "It's often assumed that individuals who've learned multiple languages simply have a natural aptitude for learning languages," said Viorica Marian, associate professor of communication sciences and disorders at Northwestern University. "While that is true in some cases, our research shows that the experience of becoming bilingual itself makes learning a new language easier."

Amazingly, this applies to any language bilinguals want to learn, no matter how different it is from their native ones because they can naturally transfer their language learning techniques across the board.

If you think about it, when we expose babies to multiple languages what we are really doing is helping their brains absorb the many sounds and create language learning pathways they can then access later on in life. What a tremendous gift and what a waste if we don't do our part to help their brains develop this way!

Not only are bilingual children more adept at learning new languages, but that flexibility persists for a much longer period of time than it does for a monolingual. According to a 2011 study conducted by researchers at the University of Washington's Institute for Learning & Brain Sciences, which expands on the Bilingual Baby Project we mentioned before, "the brains of babies raised in bilingual households show a longer period of being flexible to different languages, especially if they hear a lot of language at home."

In other words, if we'd like to introduce our children to a third language or they choose to learn one later on in their lives, they'll have a much easier time thanks to our decision to raise them bilingual early on.

Fascinating, no? No matter how you look at it, raising bilingual children is a win-win situation.

Bilingualism is Better for Your Heart

We could continue citing more research and studies on the benefits of bilingualism, but the truth is that, to many of us, scientific fact is just the icing on the cake. It helps to justify the struggles we might face, or to arm ourselves when we need to defend our decision to raise our children with two languages to those who don't really get it. However, for most of us already embarked on the bilingual journey, the initial spark came not from the brain, but from the heart.

The heart of a parent who so desperately needs to feel constantly connected to her child. The heart of a parent who always wants what is best for her child. The heart of a parent who wants to see himself reflected in his child.

For many bilingual households, language is the bridge to the essence of who we are and to the heart of our heritage. In my case, there is no better way for our girl to understand and love where we come from than by experiencing it for herself through our food, customs, family and the language which binds us to all of that: *español.*

We are now part of a growing segment of the population which has decided to go against the monolingual norm—and even social oppression—to give our children the gift of a second (or more) language, a connection to our heritage and an open door to explore diverse cultures.

The main reasons why we choose to raise bilingual children are usually more personal than not, but all those studies help back up our efforts. If we were just looking to improve our children's cognitive development, we could easily teach them a musical instrument or sign them up to play on a sports team, but the reasons behind our choice to raise bilinguals usually go beyond simple rationale into the personal and emotional realms.

WHY RAISE BILINGUALS?

At fifteen months, Camila started spitting out words like crazy, exactly at the same time she started daycare. And with this came our worries that being exposed to English *just* when she was starting to learn Spanish, would confuse her to the point that my husband's nightmares would become a reality. You see, ever since she was born, he has had nightmares about his daughter asking him to take her for a ride in his *troka* to the *marketa.* So you can imagine how important an issue her acquisition and fluency of both Spanish and English is in our home. We don't want her to just understand Spanish and speak back to us in English; we want her to be able to communicate with her grandparents, aunts, uncles and cousins in Mexico and El Salvador in *their* language. We don't want her to feel embarrassed because she speaks Spanish but speaks it differently.

By the time she had turned three, Camila had a long distance relationship with everyone in her family, except for her *mamá* and *papá.* I always feel guilty that, not only will she be an only child, but she'll also be deprived of knowing what it is to visit *la casa de la abuela* for lunch every Saturday, to have wild sleepovers with her *primas* or to just have multiple hands on deck to lovingly care for her at a moment's notice. Her first trip to El Salvador when she turned three was not only an immersion in language, but an immersion in *familia.* In this case, the two are intertwined.

From the moment we got to my mother's house, Camila was putting the new words in her vocabulary to good use: *tía, prima, primo, abuelita, abuelito.* All words she had previously known merely as concepts, not concepts I'm sure she could even grasp at her age. She had seen and met them all before—except for her one-year-old *primito*—but she was too young to retain the relationships from a distance. To my surprise, as soon as she saw them all again she immediately embraced each one with a joy that can only be bonded through blood. The next morning, the first words out of her mouth were: "*¿Dónde están mi tía y mis primos?*" Just like that, she had a family. And they all speak the same language she speaks at home. The language she associates with warmth, safety and pure love.

That was when I realized that by immersing her in Spanish, we had not only gifted her with the mighty brain of a bilingual, but we had also given her the chance to be truly connected with her family and her heritage.

As you can see, my own reasons are actually a bit simplistic, but from the heart.

MY REASONS FOR RAISING A BILINGUAL CHILD

Comfort. This is the most selfish of all my reasons, but the reality is I am most comfortable speaking in Spanish, and I want my daughter to be equally comfortable speaking to me in Spanish as well.

Camila is four at the time of writing this book and her own comfort level varies depending on the situation she's in and the amount of exposure she's had at that time. Since she's currently attending an all-English Montessori school, I find that her language of play is English and it takes a while for her to make the switch back to Spanish when I pick her up. But, once she gets going and her brain picks up that she's with *mamá*—and, admittedly, with some prodding from me!—she switches back to mostly Spanish, to that language comfort zone we have created for ourselves.

Connection with *familia*. Most of our immediate family lives in Mexico and El Salvador. I want my girl to have no inhibitions when communicating with her *abuelos, primos y tíos.* They are already separated by distance and time; they don't need a language barrier as well.

So far our efforts have paid off since she's been able to fully embrace not only her family's language, but also their food, customs and traditions in both countries. She will continue to be *la prima gringa,* but her bilingual skills have even proven to be a source of inspiration and admiration from our loved ones.

Opening doors and a world of opportunities. There's no doubt that speaking two or more languages, especially Spanish, is a much needed 21st Century skill. I have the gift of that skill in my hands, why wouldn't I pass it along to my daughter as early as possible?

I can clearly see how all of the important milestones in both my professional and personal life have been been enhanced, or even made possible, because of the uniqueness of my cross-cultural and bilingual life. I have a unique knack for understanding the American way of life, the Hispanic/Latino culture in the United States, the Latino culture south of the border and all the ways in which they intersect. It's the way I view the world and am at ease in all those scenarios. I want to share that unique perspective with my little one and have it be one of the many life scenarios which shape her future.

No regrets. When speaking to someone who is a native Spanish speaker, but is hesitating about whether or not they should pass Spanish along to their kids, I usually use my number one fear tactic on them. I tell them to fast forward to when their child is eighteen-ish and figures out by himself how much of an asset it would have been in his life's toolkit if he could say he was a fluent Spanish speaker. Maybe he wants to travel to Latin America; or he lost a great opportunity to a bilingual candidate; or maybe he just met the girl of his dreams and she only speaks Spanish. I ask them to realize that at that precise moment their child will turn around and blame them for not speaking Spanish to him when the time was right and the brain ripe. You don't want to be in that position of regret when there's no more turning back time to give this gift to your child.

My friend and fellow blogger Yvonne Condes, the daughter of Mexican immigrants and mother of two boys, is one of those people who regrets not being brought up bilingual. "I wish I spoke fluent Spanish," Yvonne openly shares with us. "I understand that my parents had their reasons for not speaking Spanish to me and to my siblings, but it's always something that's bothered me. They spoke to each other, but not to us. All of my cousins speak Spanish and many of my friends, and I feel like I'm missing something profound."

Are these the words you want to hear your child say to you when she is older? The time is now; the sooner the better. No regrets.

ROXANA SPEAKS OUT
ABOUT THE BENEFITS OF BILINGUALISM

I KNOW BILINGUAL IS BETTER BECAUSE I'M LIVING PROOF OF THAT. AT THIRTY-NINE years old and with a twenty year long career in journalism behind me, I can indisputably say that my bilingual abilities have come into play in each and every single one of my jobs. In fact, none of the jobs I've held would've been an option if I didn't speak, write and read both Spanish and English proficiently. From my first job as a reporter for *The Miami Herald* where, even though I wrote in English, I spent a lot of time reporting and interviewing in Spanish, to my current job as a staff writer for Mamás Latinas where I go seamlessly from writing in English to writing in Spanish throughout the entire day, my bilingualism has always put me in a position of privilege—both in terms of options and compensation. I know for a fact that in several of my jobs I've been offered a higher salary than my monolingual counterparts solely based on my bilingual abilities. Think about it, hiring a bilingual writer is the equivalent of hiring two writers. While I've gotten paid more for being bilingual, the companies hiring me have saved more by employing only one person. As a Turkish proverb wisely states, "One who speaks only one language is one person, but one who speaks two languages is two people."

But monetary compensation hasn't been the only benefit of being bilingual. As a journalist, being able to speak the language of those I'm interviewing has allowed me to put my subjects at ease and help them open up in a way they wouldn't have otherwise. While I have the utmost respect for interpreters, I've seen with my own two eyes how having one while reporting a story or conducting an interview can slow down the flow of the dialogue—not to mention the nuances and emotions that can be lost in translation.

Speaking of translations, a collateral benefit of being fully bilingual has been my ability to make extra money as a translator. I say collateral because I never studied to be a translator nor did I ever have any intention of being one. But, because I've pretty much done it throughout the entire length of my career as a journalist (interviewing somebody in Spanish for an English publication or TV station, for example), I decided to start offering my services as a translator when I chose to become a stay-at-home mom after Vanessa was born. The option of making extra money without leaving my house was a godsend and the practice opened up the door for me to get a full-time job as a translator in the middle of the recession. In addition, I'm one of those rare translators who has no problem translating from English to Spanish or from Spanish to English. Most bilinguals dominate one of their languages more than the other and, therefore, tend to only be able to translate from either English to Spanish or from Spanish to English. But because I've lived most of my life immersed in both languages and both cultures I have no issues doing both—once again, making me a more desirable employee.

The professional arena, though, is not the only one where my bilingualism has played a huge role. On a personal level, I'm convinced that being bilingual has made me more open and accepting of others. It has shown me that there's more than just one way to see the world. It has allowed me to participate in all kinds of monolingual settings (whether English-only or Spanish-only) that would not have been available to me had I spoken only one language. Finally, being bilingual has given me a much wider range of options when it comes to forging personal relationships. From being able to communicate perfectly with a Spanish-only recent immigrant from Guatemala to having a lengthy conversation about the significance of St. Patrick's Day with an English-only fifth generation Irish-American. Like a Czech proverb says, "You live a new life for every new language you speak."

I hope you realize that I'm not tooting my own horn for the sake of showing off. I just want to make sure that you're aware of the long-term benefits of bilingualism and the kinds of doors that speaking two or more languages will open up for the rest of your children's lives. My own children are still too little to start using their bilingual abilities to their full extent, but I have already started seeing the signs of how being bilingual is better. Allow me to share one example with you.

Vanessa—five and a half years old at the time of writing this book—recently did an amazing thing that proved how bilingual

children's brains are much more flexible, as Ana has already pointed out in this chapter. My daughter is a bookworm, just like her
mom, and her little brother Santiago is turning out be the same.
Ever since Vanessa started learning how to read in English at
school—and transferring those skills into Spanish at home all by
herself!—she loves reading to her little brother. One night, Santiago chose a book in English and asked her to read it. She knows
perfectly well that her two and a half-year-old brother doesn't really speak English just yet (which has been a great tool for making
sure we continue to speak only Spanish at home, especially in light
of the fact that English permeates the majority of Vanessa's waking hours at school), so at first she said she couldn't because it was
in English. But Santiago kept on insisting. And, out of nowhere
and without even asking me, she started reading the short little
book in English and translating it to Spanish for Santiago.

At first, she would read one word and translate it into Spanish and then read another word and so on. But then, I explained
that it was probably better to read the whole sentence and translate it in its entirety—not really knowing what to expect. I mean,
the sentences were super short, but still, she was only five and a
half and she had just started to learn how to read. I must admit, I
wasn't sure she'd be able to do it. To my surprise, she did, and not
once did she get something wrong! While I have read and reread
the large amount of information which explains how bilingual children's brains are more flexible, seeing it with my own two eyes was
inspiring. I can't deny that I was truly amazed by my daughter's
capacity to find a solution to a problem so effortlessly and without making a big deal about it. In fact, I'm pretty sure she didn't
even realize the daunting task—let's be honest, translating from
one language to another while reading is no easy feat even for
an adult—she was able to accomplish in order to make her little
brother happy.

Since my children are still so young, I know our bilingual journey has only just begun. I'm really looking forward to documenting
more real life examples of how being bilingual is better.

Now it's your turn. Use the box below to write down your top three reasons for raising a bilingual and bicultural child. Be honest and real. Treasure these reasons as your family's mission statement to refer back to any time you feel any doubt about this bilingual journey.

My Top Three Reasons for Raising a Bilingual Child
1.
2.
3.

Identifying your reasons and passion points for raising your child bilingually is key to helping you choose the best method for you and your family and to commit to it as a life choice which requires lots of love and consistency.

FIVE REASONS TO RAISE BILINGUALS

ACCORDING TO THE MULTILINGUAL CHILDREN'S ASSOCIATION, THERE ARE more pros than cons to raising your kids to be bilingual. Here are few reasons to keep you motivated:

1. It is easier to learn another language from birth than it is during any other time in life—baby simply has two first languages.
2. Multilingualism has been proven to help your child develop superior reading and writing skills.

3. Multilingual children also tend to have over all better analytical, social, and academic skills than their monolingual peers.
4. Knowing more than one language helps your child feel at ease in different environments. It creates a natural flexibility and adaptability, and it increases her self-esteem and self confidence.
5. Career prospects are multiplied many times over for people who know more than one language.

NEVER GIVE UP

As much as a believer I am in bilingualism, I must admit I've had many moments when I have doubted whether or not my obsession with speaking and immersing my girl in Spanish-only during her early years would mean she'd be at a disadvantage, both socially as well as academically. As socially outgoing as my daughter is, at age two she went through a very shy and awkward stage. She wouldn't talk to anyone and she would hide behind me or turn her face from people when she was spoken to. If we went to a birthday party, she would stay on my lap until there were only a handful of kids left, and not until then would she get up and play with them. This was certainly not the girl I knew at home or at daycare, where she was 100% comfortable and herself.

To my surprise, my own reaction to the situation was to blame it on her speaking and hearing more Spanish than English and, I assumed, not feeling at ease in an all-English group environment or conversation. Who knows, maybe that was the reason, maybe not. It could have also been that she was just going through a natural shy stage she would (and did) eventually outgrow.

Two years later, Camila is an outgoing, super social and very active girl. She's perfectly at ease communicating either in Spanish or in English and she knows exactly when to use each language.

My point is that even though I was doubting whether or not her bilingualism was the cause of her shyness, we never stopped speaking her in Spanish. Never. By then I was so immersed in the topic of raising bilinguals, had done so much research and kept reading over the experts' advice on our website that I just knew, in a rational way, that everything would be okay. I knew I had to let her go through this stage. What I learned through this experience, though, is how easy it is for parents to commit to bilingualism and then experience a moment of doubt, have that doubt be fueled by ill-advice from others, and then decide to just quit.

Don't quit. Years of solid scientific research, plus word of mouth experience from those who have been successful, as well as your heart-gut feeling prove that bilingual definitely is best.

We know it is hard work and we know there are many roadblocks and potholes along the way that can make you doubt the route you've chosen. We've been there, too. As time went by my husband and I realized that we needed a bilingual family plan – a method of sorts – and we needed to be consistent about it. In the next chapter we'll explore the many methods and strategies for raising bilingual children and help you figure out which one works best for your family.

Raising a Spanglish Baby

*

AS A CHILD OF "BOTH WORLDS," YOU CAN ALMOST SAY I HAD it easy when it came to bilingualism. It's not like I tried hard to learn Spanish and English. I just did. My mother, my sister and I moved to El Salvador from Houston when I was six years old. My mom says that by then I was already perfectly bilingual. I don't think she really gave it much thought at that time; I was getting plenty of English at kindergarten in Houston and playing all day with my English-speaking neighbors. The Spanish input I received from both my parents, as well as my aunt who lived with us and the large group of party loving Latinos my parents hung out with.

The one thing my mom was very clear about was that she wanted us to attend an American school in El Salvador. The *Escuela Americana* follows a North American curriculum from kindergarten through high school, which meant I was completely immersed in English and only had one class in Spanish every day. Not much, right? Well, I still learned to read and write Spanish with no problems. How? Because I was immersed in Spanish the rest of the day and spoke it with my peers since it was our native language. English, being the minority language, had to be more strongly reinforced through school and activities.

Summers and some holidays were spent in Houston with my dad and his new family. This meant that for a couple of months each year we were practically immersed in English, and bullied into speaking it well by our stepbrothers or face the wrath of being teased.

The fact that it was an organic and almost unplanned process for me to become bilingual, biliterate and bicultural also made me naive as to the idea of needing to actually have a plan with my own daughter. The thought had never crossed my mind before conceiving her. Now I know how truly lucky I was to be given the gift of two languages—my mother did try for a third language (French), but I was way too *necia* by then!

Growing up with one foot on this side of the border and another on the other side instilled in me a confidence that allows me to feel at ease in either culture with its many traditions. A confidence built around knowing the kinks of each culture and being able to automatically navigate between the two without a thought.

Will my daughter have that same confidence? I don't have the answer yet, but at least it gives me a goal to work towards.

My experience, as described before, was very unique to me. Roxana's experience is different in the sense that she was immersed in languages by default because of her dad's job taking her family overseas, but one thing we have in common is that our parents were conscious of the importance of having us learn English as our second language. Maybe the motives and methods were different, but the intent was the same.

Based on our own experiences growing up and the experiences of those we've met during our SpanglishBaby journey, we realized that bilingual and bicultural families cannot all be painted with the same brush. Aside from the reasons we all have for exposing our kids to another language, every household is different as to how language and culture is treated within its doors.

Both Roxana and I speak only Spanish at home with our husbands. It turns out our situation is common, but it's not the most common by far. Most bilingual households are—knowingly or unknowingly—using a method known as One Parent One Language (OPOL), where one parent speaks the majority language at home and the other speaks the minority language.

Let's explore all the methods together and find which one works best for your *familia*.

MOST COMMON METHODS OF RAISING A BILINGUAL CHILD

Minority Language at Home (mL@H)

As soon as we embarked on our initial research for the launch of SpanglishBaby, we picked up the book *Raising a Bilingual Child* by author and bilingualism expert, Barbara Zurer Pearson, Ph.D., who was also one of our first Ask an Expert contributors. Through her book, Roxana and I found out that what we were organically doing at home by speaking only Spanish, all the time, actually had a name: Minority Language at Home or mL@H.

This method is self-explanatory: everyone in the household speaks the minority language at home. But it is important to point out that neither you nor your partner have to be native speakers of the target language you'll be using exclusively at home. In other words, as long as you are both fluent in the minority language—which in this country is anything other than English—this method will work for you.

Roxana has a bilingual (Spanish/English) friend who lives in the Northeast and has been using this method with her children aged ten and eleven since they were born. They are bilingual all right, but it has been a difficult road since they live in an area with virtually no Hispanic community. This means that the only Spanish her kids get is at home from her, her husband and the nanny. The result: even though her kids are bilingual, the truth is they speak English most of their waking hours. Her strategy has been to be as strict as possible about talking to them exclusively in Spanish. In fact, many times her kids will address her in English and she'll respond by asking them to repeat what they said in Spanish.

Part of the journey of raising bilingual children is knowing that, no matter how strict you are with whichever method you choose, there will always be challenging moments when you feel that you are probably just doing it all wrong. That's why it's important to be conscious of why you choose one method over another and what it takes to follow through. Analyzing pros and cons is one of the best roadmaps to success.

mL@H Pros

- Child gets constant and consistent exposure to the minority language, in this case Spanish.

Children thrive on consistency and familiarity. There's something reassuring and comforting to them about hearing one language being spoken at home all the time. It adds to the sense of warmth that a home language can bring, and even creates a sort of code that exists within the confines of *familia*. Since in this case both parents speak the same language at home, it's easier for the child to get the necessary exposure to the language in order to become proficient and fluent.

- Easy to manage and coordinate at home between all family members because the only rule is one language is spoken there all the time.

It's easier for the parents in the sense that they don't really need to have a plan at home, other than making sure the same language is spoken there all the time. Since my husband and I are both fluent Spanish speakers, all we do is be ourselves in the language we're most comfortable in. Most families that follow the mL@H method do so because the language in common is one both are the most familiar with.

- Comfort level in speaking the language between all family members is high.

Since in most mL@H homes the language of choice is the one in which the parents are most fluent, the parents feel confident and don't have to put thought or effort into speaking the language. They are just being themselves at all times. I, for one, have always admired parents who choose to speak to their children in a language they are not a native speaker of (more on this topic later in the chapter). I honestly doubt I would feel comfortable not being able to be myself, along with my *dichos*, mannerisms and such in Spanish, and having my daughter not share that with me. I love the feeling of comfort we have as a family speaking one language. At least it works for us.

Now that I've painted such a pretty picture of mL@H, I've got to admit that there are always disadvantages to any method, and I've experienced all of these myself.

mL@H Cons

• Minimal exposure to the majority language at home.

This is probably the number one fear of parents using the mL@H method because they feel that the child will be so immersed in the minority language that he will be "behind" in his English language skills. Although this is part of the natural progression of bilingual language acquisition—when children speak in one language more than in the other at certain phases of development—what's important to keep in mind is that you're building a solid foundation in Spanish so that a child's Spanish skills are well established by the time English starts taking over his senses.

Because I was aware my daughter wasn't getting enough exposure to English at home, I decided to pass up the opportunity to enroll her in a Spanish full immersion preschool. It was an opportunity many wish for in their cities, and it can seem like a contradiction because I encourage everyone to seek out and promote dual and full immersion programs, but I didn't feel it was the right thing for us at that time because Spanish was already my girl's language of choice. The other factor is that I knew I would go to any lengths necessary to get her into a dual immersion program for kindergarten. So for us, based on our unique circumstances, this was the right decision. Every family is unique.

• Fear of child not adjusting to an all English environment.

This one goes hand-in-hand with the previous item, since this fear comes from knowing that the child hasn't received enough exposure to English from the parents. I clearly remember how nervous I was during my girl's first week at an all English Montessori preschool when she was three years old. Even though she grew up surrounded by both languages during her year at a family day care, she had never spent all day in a place where not a single person spoke or understood Spanish. She did go through a short period of adjustment while she tried to understand the code of this new place, but nothing so out of the ordinary that it set her back socially or emotionally in any way.

• There is much more access to media in the majority language.

This is especially true when English is the majority language, but the degree of access varies so much depending on the minority language. For Spanish, thankfully, it's becoming less of a struggle to find quality media and toys. While it does require thoughtful effort, research and a level of investment to acquire books, videos and some Spanish language TV channels, with a little creativity and know-how most families can create rich Spanish language media libraries at home. For example, many children's shows on popular channels have the SAP as an option in Spanish; music can now be streamed for free through many online apps; and Spanish language books are more accessible at libraries.

Now that my husband and I understand how this method works with all its advantages and disadvantages, and we also know why it's been effective for us, we are even more committed to sticking to speaking 100% Spanish at home. Where we have slacked off a bit is in the area of media exposure. We have allowed our daughter to watch some of her favorite shows in English because we feel she gets a lot of exposure in Spanish and this is one area where we can be flexible. Not something I would be doing if we were using any other method since TV, movies, music, apps, etc. are excellents tools for immersing kids in the target language in a fun and playful way. Even though methods are important and consistency is key in whatever we do, flexibility and knowing your child has to be factored in.

mL@H	
Pros	*Cons*
Child gets constant and consistent exposure to the minority language, in this case Spanish.	Minimal exposure to the majority language at home.
Easy to manage and coordinate at home between all family members because the only rule is one language is spoken there all the time.	Fear of child not adjusting to an all English environment.
Comfort level in speaking the language between all family members is high.	There is much more access to media in the majority language.

ROXANA SPEAKS OUT ABOUT THE JOYS AND PITFALLS OF ML@H

BOTH SANTIAGO AND VANESSA WERE VERY EARLY TALKERS. BY THE TIME their first birthday came around, they were both saying more than the supposed ten words considered normal for babies at eighteen months (or several months older). For a while there, it seemed like Santiago was a bit behind his sister in terms of how many words they were saying at the same age. But now that he's two and a half, I actually believe that his vocabulary is much more extensive than hers because he repeats everything his sister says just like a parrot. While I've always believed there's nothing better than speaking to your children like you would to an adult to help them develop as broad a vocabulary as possible, there's nothing like having someone who's about your same height, likes to play the same games as you and seems to understand you much better than the adults around you to help you grow your vocabulary exponentially. Such has been the case of my son Santiago who at two and a half years old is saying sentences like these:

— *Mira, tiene algo en su panza. ¿Ves?*
— *Mami, ¿cómo hacen los cohetes cuando van a la luna?*
— *Papi, quiero jugar afuera. ¿Me pones mis zapatos?*

Although we use the mL@H method at home and my children were exposed solely to Spanish during the first two years of their lives, we live surrounded by an English-only community so that's the language they've always heard outside the house. Therefore, I believe my children are prime examples of how it's a fallacy to say that it takes bilingual children much longer to speak. Yet, as proud as I am of both my children's expansive vocabulary, I'd be lying if I say I haven't worried about some of the main disadvantages of using the mL@H method. Namely, the fact that my children have minimal exposure to the majority language at home and might therefore have problems adjusting to an all English environment.

Like many parents using the mL@H method—and even in the face of all the research proving that she would be just fine—I worried about Vanessa entering preschool and knowing very few words in English. Even so, I knew there was really nothing I could do about it because changing to English at home was never an option. While I'm perfectly bilingual, I had been speaking Spanish to Vanessa for over two years by the time she entered preschool and all of a sudden switching to English simply seemed like a stretch. Not to mention that I sincerely cannot see myself speaking to my children other than in my native Spanish. Like she's done countless times before in her short life, Vanessa quickly proved there would be no need for us to change our parenting methods after just a short adjustment period at her all English preschool.

What's more, whenever other parents thinking about using the mL@H method come to me worried about how this only offers their children minimal exposure to the majority language, I use my daughter as a perfect example of how this is only temporary once they enter the English-only society we live in. Some people find it hard to believe, but my husband and I have never spoken English to Vanessa—save an occasional word here and there—and yet she's totally bilingual. In other words, English permeates children's lives to such an extent when they enter preschool that worrying about their ability to adjust to an all English environment is pretty much unfounded.

Because I had already gone through this with Vanessa, I knew I had nothing to worry about when it came time for Santiago to start a Parents Day Out program once a week at the same preschool Vanessa attended. In fact, we were pretty lucky to get the same teacher Vanessa had back when she was his age so there was no need to explain to her about Santiago's lack of vocabulary in English. I will say, though, that it does bother me just a tad when monolingual English speakers spend some time with Santiago and think his speaking abilities are pretty limited because they don't speak any Spanish and don't understand that in his first language I sometimes have to tell him to shut up because he won't stop talking. In the end, I know for a fact that his vocabulary in English will eventually catch up to his Spanish and one day, what I'll really have to worry about, is making sure his Spanish stays alive and well.

One Parent One Language (OPOL)

The most popular system in both Europe and Canada is one in which one parent speaks one language and the other one speaks another. There are several combinations of this method. For example, each parent speaks his or her own native (minority) language and the majority language is learned outside the home. In this case, the child would grow up with three languages. Another option is that the father speaks the majority language and the mother the minority one. Based on absolutely no scientific evidence, but on our own observations and conversations within the SpanglishBaby community, it seems as if the latter example is the most common one.

One friend of ours who has been using OPOL—although not exclusively—since her son was born, explains some of the problems she's encountered with this method. "Ideally, I'd never speak to him in English, but for some reason, when my husband is home, I feel a little weird, as if I am excluding him from our conversation." So, she ends up speaking in English. Actually this is a very common concern and probably the major roadblock for families attempting this method.

This issue is perfectly reflected in the following comment from Maria on our blog's Forums: "For us the biggest challenge is getting enough minority language input. Although I am home with the kids they still hear lots of English, including most conversations between my husband and myself since his Spanish is not fluent and so us speaking English is often most practical. Plus, in general, despite my constant efforts to search out Spanish in any and every way, shape and form, the community still surrounds us with English and I feel like it's a constant effort to keep Spanish in the mix."

I've always tried putting myself in the shoes of families using the OPOL method and find it quite hard, leading me to feel a sense of admiration for the many families who are so successful at it.

Families like that of Kayla Rodriguez, mother of an eight-year-old boy and a one-year-old girl, who decided to use the OPOL method because her husband is more fluent in Spanish than she is and he would, therefore, take over the role of speaking 100% in Spanish to the kids. Even though they faced the challenge of Dad forgetting to use Spanish all the time and resorting to English, their son received so much exposure that he now automatically replies in Spanish all the time. Kayla can proudly confirm, based on her own experience, "Parents should never give up on trying this method because, as long as you are consistent, your kids will pick up on the language quickly."

Lorena Gauthereau-Bryson, a Spanish teacher of Mexican-American heritage and mother to a one-year-old boy, chose the OPOL method because she had been interested in different language acquisition techniques and found this one allows the child to distinguish between the two languages more easily. Her biggest challenge is a fear many face: having to revert to English with her son around friends and relatives so as to not appear rude for speaking a language they don't understand. A fear that should not exist at all, since people should learn to respect that there is a reason why parents choose to have their children speak a certain language with them. Yet, I will admit that I, too, instinctively switch to English with my girl when we're with friends who only speak English. I can relate to Lorena's challenge, but in some way it's easier for me because as soon as we're home the Spanish veil goes back on no matter what.

Does it sound like this is the method that would work best for your family? Let's analyze the pros and cons and dig in a little deeper.

OPOL Pros

- Child gets constant exposure to both languages from birth.

In this child's world, bilingualism is the norm. From the day she begins to hear, she is constantly absorbing two mother tongues. The baby naturally absorbs and retains all the sounds of each language and learns to associate each one with the person who speaks it to her. What's important in this case is that the exposure to both languages is equal and consistent enough for the child to absorb the sounds and create the neural pathways for it. The second language could come from either a parent or a caregiver who spends a significant amount of time with the child.

- Each parent can speak in the language he or she is most comfortable in (assuming they are both native speakers).

If each parent is a native or fluent speaker of a different language, then each one can assume the role of being the carrier for that language. There's no need for both of them to switch to Spanish 100% of the time if one of them is actually much more comfortable speaking English, or any other language, including sign language. Language is generally the bridge to our heritage cultures, so when parents speak in their native language it's also more likely that they are transmitting cultural nuances to their children along the way. They are also creating a rich environment where all languages are welcomed, further motivating the child's receptivity.

- Child's brain quickly adapts to responding correctly to the language in which he's addressed.

One of the proven assets of a bilingual brain is how flexible it is. This flexibility is exercised from the day a child starts listening to two languages on a daily basis. The process of having to constantly decipher who is speaking to them in which language helps children develop their overall cognitive skills. There is no confusion in a child's brain when it comes to identifying the person he needs to address in whichever language since he will become adept at this skill from birth.

OPOL Cons

- Child could get too much input from one language, and not enough from the other.

This is usually the case when the parent who works more outside the home is the one using the minority language. It can also be the case if one of the parents is not completely on board with the idea of raising a bilingual child, or doesn't understand exactly how important it is for the child to receive maximum exposure to a language and just slacks off on his commitment or isn't consistent. A child needs anywhere from 50-60% of daily input to be in a particular language if she is to become fluent. This is probably the number one concern we hear from OPOL families, and it is why a family plan of action is so important.

- One parent may not be fluent enough in the language, thus not speaking it consistently.

Another major concern parents have is their lack of fluency in their language of choice and the fear of passing their non-native accent along to their child, if they have one. They feel they may be hurting their child's speech development by not providing a model for the proper pronunciation and/or accent. What's important to keep in mind here is that in the early years your enthusiasm and motivation is a huge part of what the child is receiving. Your love for the language and your ease of comfort with it will be transmitted to him. The child can then have other language models for the proper accent and such or be placed in an immersion program when the time comes. Meanwhile, don't let your level of fluency stunt your determination.

- One parent may spend less time with the child than the other, thus providing less exposure to his or her language.

This one clearly ties in with the two previous items in our list of cons, and it all goes back to the amount of exposure a child gets in each language. Unfortunately, constant exposure is key to language acquisition. However, even if the parent spends less time with the child, his attitude towards the language can greatly influence the child's need to learn it. I have a friend whose husband provides the Spanish in her home and, since he's not around as much as he'd like, their daughter has recently (at three years of age) taken huge leaps forward with her Spanish skills because she's realized that speaking the language strengthens the bond she has with her father. She is getting exposure from sitters and friends (like us!), but her connection to her dad is definitely her biggest motivator at this moment.

OPOL	
Pros	_Cons_
Child gets constant exposure to both languages from birth.	Child could get too much input from one language, and not enough from the other.
Each parent can speak in the language he or she is comfortable in (assuming they are both native speakers).	One parent may not be fluent enough in the language, thus not speaking it consistently.
Child's brain quickly adapts to responding correctly to the language in which he's addressed.	One parent may spend less time with the child than the other, thus providing less exposure to his or her language.

Time and Place (T&P)

In this method parents or other caregivers assign a specific time or place for speaking the minority language. This type of method is what's most often used in schools with bilingual programs. For example, the minority language is used in the morning and the majority language in the afternoon. Or some subjects, such as math or science, are in the minority language one school year and in the majority language the next.

This strategy refers less to family life than the other two, yet there are many families who do use some variation of this method, especially considering it's a great option for non-Spanish speakers who want their children to grow up learning two languages. However, it is also the one method that requires the most planning, consistency and attention to detail, if done consciously.

Since many families who use this method do so quite unconsciously, there really aren't many rules for this game. Most families just play around with it a little until they find a strategy that works for them, but they do need to stick to that strategy if it is to be effective.

Such is the case of María Babin, a blogger and bilingual mother of three polyglot tots who speak French, Spanish and English. Babin and her French husband have come up with a unique method of switching languages every two weeks. It sounds complicated, but it has actually been very successful for them. I asked Babin to share her story with us because I find it fascinating.

One Family's Success Story With the Time & Place Method (Interview with María Babin)

Ana: *Why did your family decide to use the Time & Place method of raising multilingual kids?*

María: I had never heard it called the T&P method, but that is indeed the method we have developed and adopted along our trilingual journey.

When we lived in the United States, we used the OPOL (One Parent One Language) method. At home my husband spoke French and I spoke Spanish, and everywhere else we both spoke English. When we moved to France, we had to make some adjustments, realizing that the children would quickly lose their English. We tried me switching from English to Spanish with the children once every other day, but it was too much mental gymnastics. We tried Sam speaking exclusively English to the children and me continuing with exclusive Spanish but, being French, Sam didn't feel natural speaking English with the children. And that's how we landed at two weeks at a time for English and Spanish between my children and me. Knowing how much mental gymnastics was involved, we felt one week would be too short, but we also felt one month would be too long. Two weeks somehow felt right because it gives us the time to transition into the new target language, which can take between two and four days, and we also have the feeling that we have been totally immersed in the language when the two-week mark comes up and it's time to make the switch.

Ana: *What has been your family's biggest challenge using this method?*

María: Our biggest challenge is being in public when we need to make the change, because there are a lot of mistakes made. We keep forgetting to switch to the new target language, so there is a lot of reminding and correcting and laughing. To someone else it must seem so odd and sometimes makes us embarrassed and slows down our switching process!

Ana: *Do you feel the T&P method has been successful? Why or why not?*

María: We started this method close to six years ago and it has worked fantastically for our family. There was one time when I forgot to make the switch and we spent an extra week in one of the target languages and there was another week just recently where we made a conscious decision to prolong our language period by one week because it had taken us several days to transition into the new target language due to the holidays. Other than that, for us it works almost like clockwork. There is something that clicks in my mind (or my children's minds) when it is Saturday and time to make the two-week switch. I can't explain it, but something about how immersed we are in the language triggers a reaction that says it's time to switch again. And usually when I have that feeling it's either Friday or Saturday. My children are now trilingual. They make mistakes, there are some things they have difficulty expressing or understanding, but they have a solid foundation in their two extra languages. They can communicate.

Ana: *Any tips for parents trying to decide if this method would work for their families?*

María: Use a calendar, if necessary, to keep you on track. Also, it's important to involve other native speakers in your family's language learning experiences because, otherwise, your children will learn to understand and communicate with you, but may have a harder time with others because of differences in accent, pronunciation, vocabulary, etc.

María Babin's Time and Place story is definitely very unique, and it took her family some trial and error before they got it right. What's encouraging is that their children are now trilingual.

Babin does have the advantage of being a native speaker of her languages. Non-native speakers should definitely consider enrolling their kids in some sort of bilingual education program in school to make that the time and place where their kids learn Spanish. We'll be exploring more about bilingual education in the following chapter, but for now we'd like to offer some extra help for non-native speakers raising bilingual kids.

HELP FOR NON-NATIVE SPEAKERS

It seems like more and more parents are taking it upon themselves to find a way to raise bilingual kids even if they are monolinguals or non-native speakers of the language they choose for their child (for the purposes of this book, we'll continue to refer to that language as Spanish).

There isn't one clearly defined strategy for non-native speakers to use, but their best tool would be a dual or full language immersion school for their kids. This will pretty much be the road of least resistance with the best guarantee of success.

Regardless of how non-natives decide to immerse their children in Spanish, there will be challenges and fears along the road. If you are already determined to immerse your child in a second language, we urge you not to let those challenges undermine you because you've already done the hardest part: deciding.

We asked some of our non-native speaking readers about their biggest struggles and challenges while raising a bilingual child in a language that is not their first language, and we were struck by the authenticity of some of their answers:

- "Not having friends or family around to reinforce the language!"
- "Baby talk! My instinct is to speak English to my six-month-old daughter. I really have to focus to speak Spanish all the time."
- "My biggest struggle is not understanding what she and her friends are saying to one another."
- "I'm teaching him Italian, but I don't have many friends that can help with pronouncing some words. But I don't care; we're both learning together!"

- "Not speaking Spanish myself so not knowing if his babbling includes Spanish words as well as English ones. I am trying to learn, but he is spending four hours a day at nursery and picking it up much quicker than me, I should imagine."
- "Staying true to the language… not code-switching and ending up back in all English."
- "Talking to my babies in my second language feels like talking to the houseplants."
- "I would say not having family to reinforce, or ask questions and definitely sticking to Spanish and not ending up back in English."
- "Not being able to read to him fluently in Spanish. I am what you call a "word caller" in Spanish. I can read it, but I barely know half of what I'm reading."
- "In emergencies or stressful situations or ones I haven't planned for, my instinct is always English."
- "I have been surprised by the unsolicited criticism. I'm tired of feeling the need to defend my decision to people who don't understand bilingualism and how it works. I even have a few family members who get angry with me because we can't have a three-way conversation since I only use Spanish with my daughter and refuse to switch to English regardless of where we are or who we are with. Observing how well my girl communicates in both languages at three years old, I'm learning better how to not care what others think."

These comments mirror the range of questions we've received on this topic for the "Ask an Expert" section of the SpanglishBaby blog. There is a clear common thread among the questions from non-native speakers raising bilingual children, which is why we've come up with a list of the top three questions and concerns raised by non-native speakers raising bilinguals.

- Should I speak to my child in a language which is not my native language?

This is truly a gateway question that can make or break a parent's determination to raise a bilingual child. The fear behind this question lies in both the commitment necessary to switch over to speaking in a language which doesn't flow intuitively, as well as not knowing if the effort will turn out a positive outcome for the child's fluency in the language.

Karen Nemeth, one of the SpanglishBaby experts, specializes in language acquisition and declares that, "a child can't develop true bilingual fluency unless he's exposed to rich, varied, interesting language through conversation, books, stories, songs, rhymes and games." Research shows that this exposure needs to make up about 50% of a child's waking hours; and it's not enough for children to just hear a language, they must actively participate in that language by conversing, singing and producing it.

If a non-native speaks to her child in a language which is not her own and the child is exposed to the language with rich interactions for at least half of her waking hours, she will surely learn it. However, Lori Langer Ramirez, bilingual educator and a SpanglishBaby expert, tells us, "...it will be important to immerse the child with language opportunities such as playgroups and academics with fluent speakers to keep the language fresh and maintain a connection to the sounds and syntax of the language. You can supplement your child's acquisition of the language (once she gets a little older, perhaps) with online resources like videos, podcasts and other web based tools in the target language."

Basically, the short answer is yes, you should speak to your child in a language which is not your own if you have the determination and will to expose him to said language as much as possible.

- How do I build proficiency in my non-native language to help my child become bilingual?

Ellen Stubbe Kester, Ph.D., a bilingual speech language professional, encourages non-natives to build their level of proficiency as much as possible because the richness of the language you speak to your child does matter. She states that, "... if you are using a very limited vocabulary with your daughter in Spanish, your daughter will have a limited vocabulary in Spanish."

The same rules apply to both you and your child; input drives output. The more Spanish you hear and read, the more your vocabulary will grow. Hence, Dr. Stubbe Kester goes on to recommend six approachable ways to improve your level of Spanish proficiency:

1. Use online and computer language programs.
2. Many libraries host conversation programs for people learning English as a second language. Find someone who speaks Spanish and set up *intercambios* where you speak English one day and Spanish another day.
3. Check out and read Spanish children's books from your local library.
4. Write down all of the actions, objects, and descriptors you want to say during your days with your child. Look them up at night and make cards to tape onto objects.
5. Go volunteer in a young bilingual classroom.
6. Immerse yourself in the language in a Spanish-speaking country (wouldn't we all love that!)

- Will my bilingual child pick up my non-native Spanish accent?

Accents are always a huge topic of conversation when it comes to non-natives teaching their children a language which is not their own. The best response here is that what's of real importance is not whether the child has an accent or not, but whether they have an opportunity and motivation to use the language. Barbara Zurer Pearson, Ph.D. encourages parents saying that, "As long as you are not the ONLY Spanish model the child ever has, he will be very unlikely to pick up your accent, and he will probably end up eventually correcting your errors."

So if you are fluent and comfortable with the language, the only thing to worry about is making sure you are not the only Spanish model the child ever has.

Pearson goes on to add, "Remember, as a language model for your child, you are not only providing new words and grammar; by speaking Spanish with him, you are creating an environment where Spanish is welcome all the time. That gives the child more time to practice and consolidate what he's learning. And you are demonstrating that Spanish is a language worth learning. This adds to his motivation to learn the language. Those are very big gifts you are giving your child."

Chelsea Kyle is a non-native Spanish speaker and single mom to a preschool age boy. She has decided to speak only in Spanish to her son, even though she does worry about her pronunciation and how that could affect his Spanish abilities. She tells us that she sets her fear at ease by recognizing that, "One great thing about Spanish is that there is no "correct" dialect — if I can get my point across to a Spanish speaker of any nationality, I can proudly say that I'm fluent. Isn't that the ultimate purpose of language?" Kyle goes on to say, "As far as how my Spanish sounds to native speakers (and how I sound to my son compared to how his father and grandparents sound), the truth is that I'll never know! I can't hear my own accent, so being preoccupied with whether or not I have one is futile."

She makes an excellent point, and one I hadn't even thought of: ignorance to your accent is bliss!

WHICH METHOD IS BEST?

You are the only one who can decide which method of raising a bilingual child is best for your family. As we've said, every family's situation is so unique and special, and there are so many circumstances to consider, that the best way to choose what works for you is to sit down and create a family plan.

Things to consider when creating a family plan:

- Level of fluency and comfort from each member of the family who will be an integral part of the child's life and provide significant language input.
- Resources available to immerse the child in a rich language environment. For example, can you hire a Spanish-speaking nanny? Can you travel regularly to a Spanish-speaking country?
- Availability of dual or full immersion programs in your hometown.

Another element to consider is that none of these methods seems to be fail-proof and, although consistency is important, flexibility is even more so. Even if you start with one method, who's to say that a few months down the road you won't realize another method might work better for your family or for your current situation?

My husband and I started out with a strict commitment to try as hard as we could to only expose our daughter to Spanish at home and in daycare. Any media time and books we exposed her to were always in Spanish. When she turned four years old, we started becoming a lot more flexible and allowing her to choose whether she wants to be read to in Spanish or English, or which language she prefers to watch her favorite movies in. We started relaxing as soon as we knew she was admitted into a dual language program for kindergarten because we now feel like her bilingualism will be guaranteed. Now our biggest commitment is to continue to nurture her love, and need for connection to the language and the culture it ties into.

Just like us, many families will end up using a combination of these strategies and adapting them along the way. I strongly believe your access to some form of bilingual education will make a huge difference in the approach you take. For example, maybe the OPOL method is best for your family, but Dad is the Spanish speaker and he just can't spend enough time at home to provide sufficient language input for the kids. In this case, the OPOL method would be greatly complimented by the child being immersed in Spanish in a school setting. Knowing that at age five (or even earlier, if you can find a bilingual daycare or preschool) your child will be learning to read, write and communicate in Spanish 90% of the time he is in school will be a huge mental relief that will allow your family some flexibility and ease with whichever method you choose.

We do, however, urge you to come up with some type of plan as early in your child's life as possible and stick to it as much as you can. As we have already said and will continue to reiterate in this book to drive the point across, it is never too late to raise a bilingual child, but it's to your advantage to start as early as possible to maximize the effectiveness and make it even "easier" for you and your family. No matter which strategy you choose, or your level of fluency, the following advice is useful for all bilingual families.

THREE STRATEGIES PARENTS RAISING BILINGUAL CHILDREN CAN USE AS SOON AS THEIR CHILD IS BORN—OR EVEN IN THE WOMB!

1) *Habla, habla, habla!* Researchers have found that the amount of exposure to a language does matter. Meaning, the more a baby hears the sounds of a particular language, the larger his vocabulary in that language will be.

Talk to your baby all the time in Spanish, or your target language, even if you think she has no idea what you are saying; she's absorbing every little sound and they will be the building blocks to her own speech acquisition. Reading and singing in Spanish will also enrich her bilingual environment and get her used to hearing books and songs in Spanish.

You can also organize playdates with other Spanish-speaking *amigas* with babies so that your kids listen to the chatter in Spanish while you're all entertained.

2) **Have a plan, be consistent and stick to it.** The personal strategies parents choose to raise their children to be bilingual are fundamental to creating a rich and consistent environment for learning multiple languages. As a couple, de-

cide early on which of the proven methods to raise a bilingual child you will use in your home: Minority Language at Home (mL@H), One Parent One Language (OPOL), or Time and Place (T&P).

Once you decide, make a game plan and stick to it to create familiarity and consistency in the baby's environment. For example, if the dad will be the Spanish speaker, he will always be the Spanish speaker, *sin excusas*.

3) Commit to your decision. Studies also show that the parents' desire to raise bilingual children is of utmost importance. Committing to the bilingual journey requires a real passion and desire to follow through. Be sure of what your reasons are and let that passion filter through your daily actions to ensure a fun and immersive bilingual home environment for your baby.

The research is clearly on our side; we have no excuse not to promote bilingualism for our kids as soon as they are born. Just think about it, they have no idea of the gift you are giving them and of the incredible ways it will manifest as benefits in their lives, and the best part is they can't even complain or argue against it… yet.

THE BILINGUAL REBELLION STAGE

So you've committed to the decision to pass on your native language to your child. You have your ideal method and family plan all figured out.

You read to him in Spanish when he was in the womb and inundated the house with the sounds of Juanes and Celia Cruz.

You sang to him the *nanas* and *canciones de cuna* your *mamá* and *papá* sang to you.

You talked to him non stop in Spanish; all the time, all day to make sure he knew it.

And then his first words start coming out: *Mamá. Papá. Agua. Hola. Bebé.*

You're ecstatic. He's speaking *español*!

And then words start becoming sentences and more and more of those words start turning into English, and slowly he stops responding to you in Spanish.

Do you panic? Did he lose his Spanish because of the all English daycare? Did he watch Diego and Dora one too many times in English? Did he not have enough Spanish-speaking friends?

No need to panic. You did it all right. This is actually a very natural progression of his language acquisition where he is choosing which language to use at which time. He's also demonstrating a grasp of both languages from the brain of a true bilingual.

Excellent, but you really do want him to respond to you in Spanish because that was the end goal. Right?

If you find yourself in this situation, do not worry! It's not impossible to reverse.

So, what to do if your child refuses to answer you in Spanish or whichever other minority language you use?

Simple Tips to Use When Your Children Refuse to Respond in Spanish

- Focus on the easy stuff—what they already know—and always praise them and then praise them a little more for remembering a word or for the flawless pronunciation.

- When moving on to the more difficult stuff—what they don't already know, but you want them to learn—turn the whole thing into a *juego*. So, for example, if your daughter knows the word for a certain thing, but can't remember it, try giving her a hint, the first sound or syllable. You'll be cheating, but your help will truly boost her self-confidence and she won't be afraid to try saying the word, once you get her started.
- If it's a completely new word or your child has completely forgotten it, say the word loudly and clearly and ask him to repeat it. It's a good idea to keep on using that specific word in conversation for a while so as to help him with usage and remembrance.

Tips You Should Use with Care

- Kindly remind your child to speak in Spanish, but remember that many times she will be so eager to say what's on her mind that she might get frustrated if she can't fully express herself in the minority language—which is probably her weaker one. Just be gentle in your encouragement to get her back to using Spanish, you don't want it feel like a chore.
- If she says something in English, repeat it back using the minority language. Think of this as the same thing you would with a younger child who is just learning to speak— we normally correct and help them expand their vocabulary by repeating the correct way of saying things, right? So, for example, if your child says in English "Can I go play with Lily?" you might say: "*¿Quieres ir a jugar con Lily?*" Again, just be careful how you do this.
- Finally—and this is kind of drastic—pretend you don't understand or refuse to answer until they use the minority language. This may or may not work with your children.

But beware: you shouldn't force the issue or it'll become a battleground, and you probably will not win. You will know better than anyone else how far to take this tactic or whether to use it at all.

A truly simple, but often overlooked, thing to remember is that you should stick to speaking the minority language no matter what. However, please keep in mind that this journey of raising bilingual children goes through all kinds of stages—depending on your kids' ages, so don't despair and keep at it!

"Mamá, yo solo hablo inglés"

When my girl turned four she quickly realized how much her speaking Spanish mattered to me. The following scenario took place one morning in the car: *"Mamá, yo solo hablo inglés,"* were the words I had been dreading for four years and that inevitably came out of my girl's mouth.

Did you catch the irony in it?

She said "Mom, I only speak English," but she said it in Spanish!

I calmly responded to her, *en español,* "Ah, ¿sí? Y, ¿por qué?" ("Oh, yeah? Why?")

She responded, *en español,* "Porque cuando estoy sola solo hablo en inglés." ("Because when I'm alone I only speak English.")

Okay, fair enough. Right? It still bugged the heck out of me, and I'll tell you why.

She was very upset with me when she told me this. It had been a rough morning for her and we were already running late to preschool. We were in the car when this lovely conversation occurred and she was not in a good mood at all. So, she hit me where she knew it would hurt.

For the last month her English had clearly taken off and she had been using it more and more at home. I am thrilled that she is at a great bilingualism stage where she can handle both languages well. She was going to an all English Montessori school and spent a good chunk of her day there, so it was to be expected she'd be using English when she played, sang and talked about school related things.

However, both my husband and I had hit the panic button and had been telling her more and more at home that we only speak Spanish. We'd been repeating it a lot, so much so that she'd obviously grasped that it's a passion point for me. This became clear when she told me she only speaks English; like that, so out of the blue, and while speaking Spanish.

Was I crazy to think we'd hit the rebellion point or were very close to it?

My New Plan of Action

So after that, I stepped back and reevaluated our approach to the Spanish at home rule. After all, as Barbara Zurer Pearson points out: "It's a war you're not going to win." I need to be careful not to turn speaking Spanish into a mandate, but rather something she wants to do. I need to make it so much a part of her life that she, all on her own, will not let go of it. So I came up with the following plan of action based on our new circumstances.

- Continue speaking to my daughter only in Spanish at home. All the time. No exceptions.

- When she does reply in English, I will rephrase what she said in Spanish and encourage her to repeat it. I will read to her a lot more and in Spanish. She's getting plenty of exposure to English language books at school.
- Hang out more with our Spanish-speaking *amigos* which we have plenty of, but who live all over the Greater L.A. area, and it's getting harder and harder to meet up as often as we'd all like.
- Skype a lot more frequently with her *tía*, *prima* and *abuelita* in El Salvador and family in Mexico. She adores her cousin who's two years older than her. They've spent quality time together both in El Salvador and Mexico over the years. Every time I tell her *"Si no hablas español, no vas a poder platicar con tu prima,"* ("If you don't speak Spanish, you won't be able to talk to your cousin.") she immediately switches to Spanish. That's my Ace right there.
- Remember that she will be attending a dual language immersion program and I can take it easy knowing at least half of her day will be in Spanish no matter what I do.
- Travel to Mexico and El Salvador more often! I am lucky that I've carved out a life where I can take my laptop with me anywhere and work from there. It does have its implications, but it's worth it.

Now it's your turn. What is your plan of action for when your child enters the bilingual rebellion stage? Write it down in the box below and keep it as a reference and reminder for when you need it so you will be able to respond clearly and affirmatively.

MY PLAN OF ACTION
FOR THE BILINGUAL REBELLION STAGE

Once you've tackled the pros and cons, created your family's plan of action and decided on the best method for raising a bilingual child—and for handling the rebellious stage that often accompanies this process—you should investigate which options you have for enrolling your child in one of the many options for a bilingual education program. A full or dual language immersion program starting as early as preschool, but no later than kindergarten, can be your clearest path to bilingual success. Follow along with me to the next chapter where we break down the past and current state of bilingual education in the United States, and we look forward to a future that is brighter and more successful with each passing day.

Bilingual Education

※

I HAVE TO ADMIT I AM VERY NAIVE. I GREW UP THINKING EVERY one WAS either born speaking more than one language, learned a second language in school like I had in El Salvador, or had the burning desire to learn one somehow.

I also naively thought that every parent in the United States would be thrilled at the opportunity to have a second language taught in elementary schools or, even better, in preschools.

It wasn't until after we launched SpanglishBaby, and started delving into the politics and all the different methods of bilingual education, that I realized how big of an issue it is among the most fervent patriotic nationalists, especially if we're talking about learning Spanish—the language of "immigrants," in their view. In fact, in a 2007 speech to the National Federation of Republican Women, former House speaker Newt Gingrich dared to speak for all Americans when he proclaimed, "The American people believe English should be the official language of the government. We should replace bilingual education with immersion in English so people learn the common language of the country and they learn the language of prosperity, not the language of living in a ghetto."

I too am American by birth and, unlike Mr. Gingrich, I believe that a nation of bilinguals, where a diversity of tongues and cultures are embraced, is the true movement towards prosperity. Bilingual education immersion programs can be a path to get us there—to a nation of culturally rich, intellectually motivated, respectful and global citizens.

However, in many aspects bilingual education is still misunderstood and the progress being made towards the growth of effective programs is moving at a slow pace. Rhetoric like the aforementioned comment spewed by Newt Gingrich is partly responsible for this slow growth and definitely not an isolated sentiment. In fact, the anti-bilingual education movement has very deep roots.

A BRIEF HISTORY OF BILINGUAL EDUCATION IN THE UNITED STATES

Bilingual education throughout the last three centuries has been a focal point of political discussion centered around civil rights issues, and speaking any language other than English was even identified as a "threat to national unity that increased the risk of insurrection and terrorism" during World War I and II. In this sense, the original purpose of bilingual education was to integrate and assimilate newly arrived immigrants to help them learn English as quickly as possible. There's an enduring conflict among those who believe that to become truly American, you must strip yourself of your language, customs and heritage and those who believe we can co-exist as a nation of multiple identities, all of which are fully American. The melting pot versus the mosaic.

Bilingual education has been at the center of this debate ever since the 1700s when European immigrants, mostly of German descent, arrived to this country and opened up their own schools where children were being taught in their native, non-English languages. In 1839 Ohio became the first state to adopt a bilingual education law to allow instruction in both German and English. Several states like New Mexico and Louisiana followed their lead.

However, just twenty years later, the first strong anti-bilingual education ruling came out of Congress prohibiting Native Americans from being taught in their native languages. This new law even went so far as to separate children from their parents by sending them to boarding schools where children who were caught speaking in their native tongues were punished. Language suppression as a means of social oppression was clearly being executed well into the late 1800s.

Meanwhile, in the early 1900s immigration to the United States from southern European countries continued to flood in with increasing numbers, intensifying the issue of language instruction, while at the same time adding to the controversy of assimilation. The government's response was to pass the first federal language law as part of the Naturalization Act of 1906. This unprecedented law, which standarized naturalization procedures, mandated—among other requirements—that any person seeking to become a naturalized citizen must pass an English proficiency test. What ensued a little less than twenty years later was a wave of English-only instruction laws which were enacted by a total of thirty-four states, mostly fueled by anti-immigration sentiments during World War I. These laws basically demolished the state of bilingual education at the time.

In the 1960s a new wave of immigration, this time led by Cubans who had to flee their country during the revolution, settled in Florida. Yet, unlike most immigrant groups before them, these newcomers never completely let go of their language or heritage. They quickly established private schools with instruction in Spanish, and soon thereafter opened the first dual language immersion public school in the country, Coral Way Elementary in Miami.

During the height of the civil rights movement and the continued influx of immigration, Congress passed the Bilingual Education Act (1968) to once and for all encourage native language instruction in all schools by allocating federal funds to school districts for this purpose. Most states enacted bilingual education acts of their own, or at the very least allowed native languages to be spoken in schools.

Just a mere thirty-four years later, the strides made by the Bilingual Education Act towards supporting native-language instruction alongside English were effectively repealed when President Bush's administration enacted No Child Left Behind (NCLB) in 2002. By using only English language standardized tests to measure a school's performance and threatening those schools which don't make the grade with punitive damages, NCLB has pretty much relegated bilingual instruction to the duty of making sure non-English speakers become proficient as soon as possible, usually in three years, thus eliminating their native language.

Sadly, this new approach to bilingual education under NCLB clearly ignores the fact that language acquisition is a developmental process you cannot put a due date on. The reality is that children learn better in a language they are already proficient in until they have mastered their second language and can then transfer those academic skills over.

Research data provided by Ramirez, Yuen and Ramey states that, "Spanish-speaking students can be provided with substantial amounts of primary language instruction without impeding their acquisition of English language and reading skills...The data suggests that by Grade 6, students provided with English-only instruction may actually fall further behind their English-speaking peers."

Furthermore, a 2000 Californians Together report entitled *Bilingual Schools Make Exceptional Gains on the State's Academic Performance Index (API)* found that "Children in bilingual education classes performed better on tests of academic achievement than students receiving most of their instruction in English," said Dr. Norm Gold, who conducted the study.

WHERE ARE WE NOW?

Despite the abundance of evidence to suggest that bilingual education programs which focus on complete English immersion or English as a Second Language often hinder native speakers' academic and social growth, the last decade has seen the proliferation of this kind of programs. The enactment of No Child Left Behind encouraged states like Arizona, California and Massachusetts to jump on the anti-bilingual bandwagon by passing bills to support English-only instruction in schools. In California, the state with the highest number of English Learners in the country, Proposition 227 mandated that children who spoke a language other than English at home be placed in a structured English immersion program for a period of one year. After that year, they are to be transferred to regular classrooms taught in English. Prop 227 did give parents the possibility to request alternative programs for their children, but information about these programs wasn't completely accessible. However, it is this possibility that has enabled parents to lead the current movement towards alternate dual language programs, which we'll be discussing later on in this chapter.

Melanie McGrath is the founder of the Multilingual Mania blog and the coordinator of dual immersion and transitional bilingual education programs in Southern California. She explains that in California we are currently still operating under the No Child Left Behind Law instituted by President Bush, which has forced many schools into program improvement status. "No Child Left Behind completely dismantled the previous Bilingual Education Acts that were in existence since the 1960s, and to date NCLB has not been reformed. The way in which California has interpreted NCLB has been to create an exclusively English-only accountability system." McGrath adds that although in California English Language Learners in bilingual programs can take the state assessment tests in Spanish, the state does not take any of those test scores into account within the accountability system. She claims that, "Unless federal policies and initiatives such as NCLB and Race to the Top explicitly provide guidelines to states that primary language assessments must be included in the state accountability system, our bilingual programs will continue to suffer punitive sanctions."

And therein lies the fundamental flaw in the focus of bilingual education in the United States. For so many years bilingual educators have been trying to instruct foreign language students as English Language Learners, eliminating their native languages to force them to assimilate and become proficient in one language only: English. What the system has never really taken into account are the many benefits of bilingualism itself, both for English Language Learners and their native English-speaking classmates. Thankfully, a small, parent-led grassroots movement is slowly but surely changing the way Americans view language in general. All over the United States parents from all kinds of backgrounds are be-

132

ginning to see bilingualism as an asset rather than a threat. Bilingual dual immersion schools are cropping up all over the country, and there are huge waiting lists as parents compete to give their children a chance to become bilingual. And in a country where nearly forty million people speak Spanish, it should come as no surprise that the language at the forefront of this bilingual parenting revolution is Spanish.

The Status of Bilingualism in the World vs. the United States	
World	*United States*
Worldwide more people speak English as a second language than speak English as a native language.	10% of educated people in the United States are bilingual.
50 % of all people in the world are bilingual.	Only 20% of U.S. citizens have passports and have traveled outside of the United States.
Worldwide quest to learn English is a quest for bilingualism.	Political pressure to declare English the official language.
If you can speak Spanish and English you can communicate with 80% of the people on the planet.	The United States is the major superpower in the world without being very worldly.

Source: 2-Way Cabe Day 2 Keynote, Kathy Escamilla, PhD.

All Children in the United States Should Learn Spanish

The United States of America, a nation that prides itself on being a melting pot of cultures which was built off the backs of immigrants for centuries, is, ironically, a country of monolinguals, where learning a second language has historically only been seen as a requirement to graduate high school. Cries for English-only come as a desperate attempt to preserve a notion of national identity through one language only, yet the proponents of an English-only United States fail to see the big picture scenario of a country that has always had an underbelly of Americans who feel 100% patriotic and assimilated but at the same time maintain their customs, foods, rituals and languages as a form of personal identity and nostalgia for their heritage.

As a matter of fact, many staples in the mainstream U.S. food industry which are now so "American," have been adopted from other countries: hamburgers, fries, pizza and even the burrito.

If we all stood by the Republican cries of English-only laws in education and social reforms, we would be facing a true nation of monolinguals, creating not only a disadvantage in a competitive international world, but also a population with little access to other cultures and languages.

Beyond the benefits of teaching our kids any second language, there is a real advantage to learning Spanish.

New York Times columnist and Pulitzer Prize winner, Nicholas D. Kristof, recently wrote an op-ed piece entitled *Primero Hay Que Aprender Español. Ranhou Zai Xue Zhongwen* (First Learn Spanish. Then Study Chinese.) The point he cleverly, and even bravely, makes is that even though Chinese is growing in popularity as the language of

134

choice for parents who want to give their children an educational advantage, Spanish is the language every child in the United States needs to learn. Kristof boldly states:

> "Look, I'm a fervent believer in more American kids learning Chinese. But the language that will be essential for Americans and has far more day-to-day applications is Spanish. Every child in the United States should learn Spanish, beginning in elementary school; Chinese makes a terrific addition to Spanish, but not a substitute."

In recent years, Mandarin has acquired a level of prestige for over-achieving and competitive parents who want their children to be able to fairly compete in our 21st Century's business world. However, the argument can be made that the real social and economic advantage in the United States today comes from knowing how to communicate *en español.*

FOUR REASONS WHY CHILDREN
IN THE UNITED STATES SHOULD SPEAK SPANISH

1. Spanish is the second most spoken language in the United States.

In fact, according to the latest U.S. Census Bureau numbers, thirty-four million people in the United States speak Spanish at home, making this the country with the second largest population of Spanish speakers in the world. That's ahead of Spain and second only to Mexico. Think about that for a second or two. We have more Spanish speakers here than they do in any of the countries in Latin America, except for one!

A child who does not speak Spanish is at a disadvantage when it comes to engaging in many of the day-to-day activities and interactions that make up the thread of this nation.

2. United States–Latin American relations are increasingly more closely knit.

Barriers have blurred and, no matter how high we try to build the walls, we have a co-dependent existence with our neighbors across the border. As Kristoff points out, the economies in the Latin American region were some of the few which have continued to grow during the economic crisis. Americans are travelling back and forth to Latin America, and we are doing more and more business together as the region becomes highly attractive in every sense. Our children will most likely encounter many career, business and lifestyle opportunities south of the border, and speaking Spanish will be essential.

3. Spanish is becoming a language of business in the United States.

No matter which career you choose nowadays, you will likely encounter a need to speak Spanish in the United States. Not only is it useful in daily interactions, but it is also helpful for expanding business potential and reaching a broader scope of the population.

4. Spanish is an "easy" language to learn and be exposed to in daily American life.

As Kristof points out, learning a language like Chinese is pretty much a career because of the complexities of the verbal and written language. Spanish, on the other hand, is easy to grasp, practice and put to use in every day life. There are many opportunities to engage in Spanish, to find peers to practice with, to inexpensively travel to immerse yourself in the language and to feel an immediate sense of accomplishment by using it often.

I hope there comes a day when it will be absurd to write a list of reasons to convince people of the need for children to learn Spanish at an early age. I know that if you are reading this you probably have other, more personal reasons—such as heritage, family connections, academic benefits, etc—for teaching your child Spanish. It is my hope that this list will not only reinforce your decision but also empower you to share your reasons for raising a bilingual child with others. The benefits are just so clear, which is why it is so important for our nation's education system to start paying attention to the needs of our children.

In the last couple of chapters you've learned about the benefits of raising a bilingual child and the many methods and strategies available to any willing parent. Yet, while all those methods are effective if used consistently, there's one method that is pretty much infallible and guaranteed to help children become bilingual, no matter which language(s) are spoken at home: dual language immersion programs in schools. This revolutionary bilingual education model is changing the course of bilingual education in the United States.

A BRIGHT NEW FUTURE FOR BILINGUAL EDUCATION

The United States is going through a very important transitional period when it comes to bilingual education, and the forecast appears to be bright. This brighter future is being paved by the vision and persistence of parents like you and me—yes, you! Just by reading this book you are already contributing to a movement being led by a new generation of parents who are passionate about giving their children the gift of bilingualism and who, armed with the latest research and data, are advocating for bilingual education that works for all children, regardless of immigration status, acculturation levels or the color of their skin.

Immigrant or not, native Spanish or English speaker, and all politics aside, parents around the nation are discovering that the point is for all children to be encouraged to develop their innate capabilities to learn as many languages as they are exposed to at an early age when their brain is more open to absorbing them.

The changing demographic and acculturation levels of the Latino population has contributed greatly to this shift in mentality towards how bilingual education should work and what we should be trying to achieve through our bilingual education programs.

The history of bilingual education in this country has been tightly tied in with immigration patterns. Yet according to a report from the Pew Hispanic Center, the latest Census data shows the growth rate in the Latino population is coming not from immigration, but from U.S. born children of Hispanic descent. This means that for the first time in U.S. history there is a new generation of Latinos who have already assimilated and have no need for our children to be taught English as a second language. We are a growing group of Latino parents who are proud of our language and heritage, and we are committed to raising a community of skilled biliterate and bicultural children who can communicate fluently in two or more languages. Unfortunately, the old English Language Learners programs, or even Transitional Bilingual programs—which the current Obama administration supports—won't help us achieve our goals.

This leads me to conclude that those bilingual education programs which simply exist as a means to assimilate immigrant children as quickly as possible will continue to decline. In their place, we'll see much more of a growth in dual language immersion programs because the focus of parents is now on making sure their children are as prepared as possible to be world citizens and compete in a global market.

This trend is already palpable in Texas, which now leads the nation in the number of schools with dual language programs. Texas educators and parents are leaning on the type of research put forward by academics such as Wayne Thomas and Virginia Collier, who have been studying bilingual education for over twenty years and have concluded that dual language programs are superior. These bilingual education experts believe the massive achievement gaps we're currently experiencing in the Latino community can be closed simply by using a solid six years of dual language immersion education.

As reported in their article "The Astounding Effectiveness of Dual Language Education for All," Collier and Thomas examined twenty-three different and diverse school districts under a dual language enrichment program. What they discovered was that dual language programs in all their variations close the academic achievement gap by 70-100% by the fifth grade. This leads them to advocate for dual language programs not only for English Language Learners, but also for every student. In other words, by implementing quality dual language immersion programs in school systems all over the country, we could effectively eliminate the achievement gap among Latino children while creating a nation of truly bilingual citizens at the same time.

DUAL LANGUAGE IMMERSION

So what exactly is a dual language immersion education program? A well designed dual immersion program encompasses the "best of both worlds," as the educators and experts we've interviewed over the past few years at SpanglishBaby have told us repeatedly. Extensive research both in the United States and other countries shows that students who participate in programs which allow them to add a second language to their first, whether they are language minority (i.e. Spanish) or language majority (i.e. English) students, "demonstrate higher levels of language proficiency, achievement and self-concept."

Furthermore, the immersion of English speakers into the minority language promotes "higher levels of second language proficiency," while the immersion of Spanish speakers in their native language produces "not only higher levels of their native language but also higher levels of English proficiency."

According to Biliteracy for a Global Society, a publication by NCELA (the National Clearinghouse for English Language Acquisition and Instruction), dual language education models are different from other forms of instructing English Language Learners in that:

- Language minority students are integrated with native English speakers in an environment that explicitly values the language and culture of the language minority student and that treats all students, regardless of language or ethnic background, in an equitable fashion.
- At the kindergarten and first grade levels, the target language is the status language for a significant portion of the instructional day, and English speakers look up to and are helped by the target language speakers because of their knowledge of the target language. During English time, the situation is reversed.
- Both groups of speakers are highly valued, not only the English speakers, as is the norm in most classrooms.
- Teachers are trained to treat all students equitably and to have high academic expectations for all students. Teachers are expected to communicate this equity to students in the classroom so that all students value each other, regardless of their language, ethnic, religious, or social class background.

Within dual immersion programs, there are two main versions used to accomplish the aforementioned objectives. In the education world, they are known as the 90:10 model and the 50:50 model. Most schools determine which model they're going to use depending on the school system's demographics, needs and resources.

In the 90:10 model, the amount of time spent with each language varies depending on what grade the student is in. Usually, children spend 90% of their time being taught in Spanish and 10% in English while in kindergarten and first grade. By second and third grades, the percentages shift to 80% of the time in Spanish and 20% in English. The idea is to gradually move to where students will be taught half of the time in one language and the other half in the other. This normally happens by the time the students get to fifth grade.

The 50:50 model does this from the very beginning. However, there are a few ways to actually accomplish teaching half of the time in English and the other half in the second language. Some schools do this by dividing the school day in two; others alternate languages each week. Still others teach certain subjects in English and others in the second language.

It's important to mention that the most successful ratio of English speakers vs second language speakers is 50/50. The philosophy behind this is that it promotes equity in the linguistic and environmental sense, as well as a healthy level of interaction amongst the students. The 50:50 ratio is the ideal, yet many districts need to adapt this ratio to the demographics of their community and have a hard time fulfilling the language proficiency levels in each group. Most experts agree that a 70:30 ratio is a minimum balance requirement to have enough heritage language speakers in a class to stimulate the natural second language acquisition process.

However, there are always exceptions to every rule, like in the case of the first dual language immersion Spanish classes at Franklin Elementary Magnet School, which started out with mostly native English speakers in the first two groups. Sara Quintanar was one of the forward thinking mothers who enrolled her daughter in one of the first Spanish dual language classes at Franklin. Both she and her husband speak Spanish, but up until then they had neglected to speak it consistently to their daughter. By the time she entered kindergarten she was only able to say "*dulce, por favor*" and "*hola.*" Sara's daughter could understand a few phrases, but by no means could she be considered bilingual.

"All of the other students, except for two out of the sixty, were new to Spanish as well, so the students quickly created a community. The fact that they could ask the teacher questions in English, and speak to their friends in English made the students feel comfortable," Sara tells us. "My daughter assumed that the teacher understood English, but was very surprised that she could not 'speak' it."

The first two dual language Spanish classes at Franklin during the 2009-2010 school year proved to be a huge success since the children and parents adapted well to the 90/10 model. Standardized testing doesn't begin until the second grade, so there are no hardcore statistics to prove the academic effectiveness of the program in this particular school yet. But Sara will tell you she has her own measure of success. "Immediately following kindergarten, my daughter answered a phone call from her *tía* in Guadalajara," recalls Sara, who also teaches music in Spanish to the kids at her daughter's school. "They stayed on the phone for about ten minutes, and my daughter was thrilled to finally engage in a conversation with a *tía* she knew and had met twice before, but had never been able to talk to. I could tell right then and there that the program had been a success."

Luckily for Sara, their school was able to create an effective dual language program with a lower ratio of native Spanish speakers. The school's popularity has grown so much that now they are able to meet their target ratio of native language speakers and give priority to children who speak Spanish at home. This is yet another reason to make sure your child is speaking Spanish, or another target minority language, before they enter kindergarten. Their language proficiency will give them an advantage when applying to a dual language immersion program, if you're lucky enough to have one close to home. I live in Los Angeles and have been fortunate to find many options, and even more fortunate to have been placed in our first choice. Roxana, on the other hand, hasn't been as lucky in Denver.

ROXANA SPEAKS OUT ABOUT THE LACK OF DUAL IMMERSION OPTIONS IN HER AREA

I WAS ONE OF THE FIRST PEOPLE ANA GOT IN TOUCH WITH THE GLORIOUS DAY she found out Camila had won a spot at the dual language immersion school in their neighborhood, and I was ecstatic. Yet, I'd be lying if I said I didn't feel a tinge of jealousy. You see, I live in the suburbs to the south of Denver where dual language immersion programs are as abundant as ocean waves. In other words, they're non-existent. Not that my options are any better closer to the city.

When Vanessa turned four and I started thinking about kindergarten more seriously, I began my search for dual language immersion options. Sadly, this is what I came up with: one brand new dual language immersion program about twenty miles from our home, a 50-50 immersion program even farther than that and three private dual language immersion schools—one Catholic—all just as far from our home and with tuition ranging from nearly $8,000 to over $12,000 a year per student (and I have two children, so you can do the math).

The truth is that if I had the money, I would have probably gone for one of the private schools since entrance to the other two public options—both charter schools—is not guaranteed and, like most dual language schools these days, everyone must go through the lottery process. As the date to make the choice of where to enroll Vanessa for kindergarten fast approached, my husband and I decided she would go to the highly rated all English elementary school by our house.

While I've never felt the need to justify any of the decisions I make as a parent, for those who know how important bilingualism is in my household making the decision not to drive eighty miles every day to cement my daughter's bilingual and biliterate abilities might seem kind of hypocritical or, at the very least, contradictory. This is how I respond: I know parenting is full of sacrifices, but this was one through which I wasn't willing to put not only myself but, most importantly, my five-year-old child. Twenty miles one way might not seem like a lot to some people, but when you factor in rush hour traffic and weather—we live in Colorado where weather is as erratic as I've ever seen—into the equation, it sounds more like torture to me. Plus, the schools' schedules didn't really jive with my husband's or my work schedule at all. There's nothing that I would've hated more than enrolling Vanessa in one of these schools only to pull her out halfway, unable to deal with the toll it would've taken on all of us. As anybody who has a child in a dual language immersion program can attest, one of the most important elements for this type of education to succeed is each family's commitment to staying through the entire length of elementary school.

In the end, I kept on telling myself that kindergarten is only the beginning and that Vanessa already had to adjust to the idea of going to school full-time for the first time in her life. I really couldn't fathom waking her up at 6 a.m., almost two hours before her regular wake-up time, and having her get back home twelve hours later—since she would have had to stay in the after school program until I got off work and picked her up—when the elementary school in our neighborhood is just two very short blocks from our home! I must say there's nothing that both my husband and I have enjoyed more than walking our daughter to and from school every day since she started kindergarten.

A small part of me still feels terrible about this decision, especially after visiting some of the dual language schools, but I keep on reminding myself that Vanessa's just getting started with her schooling. Incredibly, she has already started demonstrating that, like Ana stated in chapter 2, bilingualism improves reading speed and comprehension. While I worried sick about whether or not I should teach Vanessa how to read in Spanish before she entered kindergarten—based on studies suggesting it's better, and easier, for children to learn to read in their first (or dominant) language— it seems like I wasted my time needlessly. Not only has Vanessa excelled at reading (and writing too) in English, but she has blown me away by transferring the reading skills she's learned in English at school into Spanish when she's at home surrounded by a pretty large library of children's books in Spanish. The most incredible part is that she has done this pretty much by herself, thereby essentially teaching herself how to read in Spanish—dissipating a lot of the angst I had regarding this topic because I didn't even know how I was going to go about accomplishing it. Another point in favor of bilingualism!

Even so, as Vanessa gets older and her education becomes more complex, I know the onus of making sure she grows up biliterate will be on me. As a product of a dual language immersion program myself, I know full well the amazing and unparalleled benefits of this type of privileged education. Attending a British school back home in Peru where most of my instruction was in English is what single-handedly made me bilingual and biliterate. Therefore, there's nothing that I wished for more than dual language education for both my children. But, until our current living arrangement changes or until the public school system realizes the importance of bilingualism and starts offering more dual language options (or I decide to start a grass-roots movement and get other parents involved in clamoring for more dual language schools), making sure my children can not only speak but also read and write in Spanish is one more thing that will be left up to me. Luckily for them, I'm totally up for the challenge.

Our Journey Towards Dual Language Immersion

I consider myself a pretty relaxed parent who lets her daughter explore and engage in activities which interest her without much judgment on my end. I do draw the line, though, when it comes to her being a fluent Spanish speaker. No negotiations on that end. Since I know my own limits as well, I know I need to rely on an effective bilingual education model to help with our goal of raising a bilingual and biliterate child. Not only because I am not cut out to or cannot afford to stop working and homeschool her, but because I want her to be surrounded by all the cultural richness that comes from being part of a diverse immersion environment.

Dual language or two-way immersion programs promote complete bilingualism, biliteracy and multicultural awareness.

I completely grasped this the day my daughter and I made it out to the twentieth anniversary celebration of the dual language program at Grand View Boulevard Elementary in Los Angeles. As part of the festivities they had put together a show where all the kids from pre-K through fifth grade performed different dances and songs from various countries in Latin America. Everything from salsa to traditional Mexican dances from many regions to the cumbia of La Bala from El Salvador and merengue. My girl sat mesmerized in the front row and I could see her little hips and shoulders naturally and rhythmically sway to the different tunes. Many months later she's still telling me she wants to go to the school where the kids dance. Now, can you imagine the cultural impact if you are one of those kids? Dual immersion programs are about two languages and two cultures and being open to more.

Just three years ago when we launched the blog, I visited what was then Benjamin Franklin Elementary school in the

Glendale Unified District in California. We wrote a series of posts about this school and the district because they were one of the few in the Los Angeles County area to successfully implement dual language, or two-way, immersion programs. This particular school, Franklin, had just launched with the German program and was already getting huge requests to launch Spanish and Italian programs. Thanks to the parents and the district working closely together, the school has now become so wildly popular that in 2011 it received funding to become a language magnet school.

Beautiful for them, but not the best news for us since we had moved to the Glendale district two years ago just so that our daughter would be eligible to go to Franklin. We had to join the hundreds of parents praying that luck was with them the day the public lottery was held to fill the forty-eight or so spots available in the Spanish Dual Language program at what's now known as the Franklin Elementary Magnet School.

As you can imagine, we really wanted to get into this school. Not only because it's a four minute drive from our house, but also because the quality of parent and teacher involvement is amazing. Since the entire school is now a language magnet school (German, Italian, Spanish and French), every single parent there is completely invested in making the program a success, and many have emotional and cultural ties to their children being educated in their native languages.

The way the lottery works in this district is that the first priority goes to siblings. Every single sibling has the right to be placed. Once those slots are taken (and apparently there are a lot of siblings entering this year, much to our chagrin), the second priority goes to balance out the proportion of native English speakers versus Spanish speakers to maintain the 50/50 proportion, as much as possible.

My girl had to attend a language proficiency test in order to place her in the fluent category. I was so nervous because I felt this was our best chance at securing a spot. Thankfully, she passed as fluent, marking this as a milestone of the first time her bilingual skills opened up a door for her.

Sitting in that room on the day of the lottery, waiting to see if our name had made the list, was very intense. In the room there were three representatives from each of the three magnet schools in our district. Basically, the computer guy (that's what they called him!) hit the enter button in our presence to randomize and select the names for each school and each program. Then, the machine spit out sheets of paper with the lists, which were handed out to each school's representatives. We were then given the green light to rush over to the school we had applied to and tell them our child's name so they could seal our fate.

I told our school's representative my daughter's last name and she said, "I'm sorry, she didn't make it, but don't despair because she can be added to the wait list." I began to shake and my heart just fell. Like, seriously fell. My eyes teared up, and I was about to walk away when the school's immersion program's coordinator asked me to repeat the last name again. I did, and I spelled it out. My girl's last name is Dutch and does not sound at all like it is spelled. She looked again, and there Camila was on the list! Now I really teared up with joy!

My head is already spinning with all the ideas I have for documenting and sharing my family's life from inside the classroom. I plan on being a class volunteer and will be as involved as possible with this amazing group of parents and teachers. I want to tell the story of dual language immersion from the inside in the hopes of inspiring others to rally for dual language programs in all schools.

Why Aren't Dual Language Immersion Programs an Option at Every School?

Unfortunately, the lack of an adequate proportion of speakers of each language is not the only reason some of these programs have failed. Education issues involving Spanish seem to create more controversy than any other foreign language, and we've found that the reasons for this are quite obvious. In the end, it all boils down to immigration and how for many Americans it represents a threat to their national identity.

As Univision's anchor, Jorge Ramos, told us in a 2009 interview, "In the United States, many people have the wrong idea that what unites the country and its people is the language, when the reality is that it's all about its values, its laws, its attitudes and the fact that they have always accepted people that come from all over the world."

According to the educators we've interviewed, there's a lot of ignorance surrounding the methods for teaching English Language Learners, dual immersion programs and bilingual education in general.

"I think bilingual education is criticized because some Americans are such isolationists and can't see the importance of learning another language," says Sisi Martinez Purfield, a bilingual kindergarten teacher with eighteen years of experience. "I think that there is also racism involved, *les gusta el pan pero no el panadero.*"

The truth is that many of those who oppose bilingual education don't really have expertise in this field to begin with and others base their criticism on the results of some bad programs that didn't accomplish either of their objectives. *En otras palabras,* they neither helped English Language

Learners acquire English nor did they help them maintain their heritage language, Spanish.

According to Marcelo and Carola Suárez-Orozco, authors and co-directors of the immigration studies program at New York University, "The best results come from dual immersion classes, in which students learn half the time in English and half in their native language, usually Spanish, with half the class being native English speakers and the other half native Spanish speakers."

It is easy to see why students enrolled in dual immersion programs succeed and end up being not only bilingual and biliterate, but also bicultural. What more can someone interested in raising bilingual children ask for?

Unfortunately, a lot because there simply aren't enough of this type of schools available for our children. According to the Center for Applied Linguistics, as of October 2011 their directory listed four hundred two-way immersions programs in thirty states, including Washington D.C. These programs serve students in Pre-K through high school. That number is insanely low if you consider that the total number of public schools in the nation during the 2009-2010 school year was 98,817. We're saying that a measly 0.4% of the public schools in the United States offer a dual language immersion program, when, according to the latest Census data, 11.2 million school-aged children (between the ages of five and seventeen) speak a language other than English at home.

PARENTS CAN MAKE A DIFFERENCE

And this is where we all come in. If 21.1% of all children in the United States between the ages of five and seventeen speak a language other than English at home (12.1% are

Spanish speakers), then it's safe to assume there is a mass of people with an interest in making our public education system work for the academic language needs of our children.

As daunting as the task of advocating in your local school district is, the reality is that many of the dual language programs available in public, magnet and charter schools exist because of parent-led movements.

In 2011, the Los Angeles Unified School District drew up a three-year plan to strengthen dual language immersion programs from kindergarten through twelfth grade. They saw the need because for years they had been losing enrollment in the district to neighboring districts, charters and private schools. But during the recession many middle class parents gravitated back towards the few dual language programs in LAUSD and, thus, have helped revitalize the district.

Angelina Sáenz, M. Ed., is the lead teacher for the Aldama Elementary Dual Language program in LAUSD. She tells us that in the case of Aldama Elementary, middle class families who bought property in the working class neighborhood of Highland Park, wanted their children to attend a school in their neighborhood, learn a second language, experience the cultural, linguistic and economic diversity of Highland Park and have the rigor of a Dual Language curriculum. Sáenz is proud to share that the parents, "... lobbied the Los Angeles Unified School District to find the space and teachers to open up a dual language program, and the very successful program is now in its fourth year of implementation, with waiting lists at all grade levels and an enthusiastic community of prospective families."

However, parent involvement doesn't end there. In order for dual language programs to be truly effective, they need the intense and hands on participation of parents at every level. "Parents in the Aldama dual language program have assumed leadership in the PTA and, through aggressive fundraising, have brought services and programs to our school that didn't exist before." According to Sáenz, "These programs have improved the quality of the educational experience for the entire school community, not just dual language students, and have built up the community by organizing family activities where all can participate."

Parents have learned that they must advocate for children not only during the early education years, but also at the middle school and high school levels, where dual language programs usually disappear. "It was a parent-led movement that envisioned a successful pipeline (K-12) for Dual Language students in LAUSD. Parents were part of the planning process to bring dual language back into Mark Twain Middle School, which is now in its second year," says María Alamillo de Ramírez, mother of three children in dual language programs in Los Angeles Unified District. Alamillo further emphasizes that, "when parents are passionate about their children's education, they come together to create change within a system that is often resistant."

Whether we lead a grassroots movement to incorporate a dual language program in our schools or quietly make a loud statement just by enrolling our children in the schools that do offer them, we are making a difference in growing the opportunities for more and more programs to be developed.

SpanglishBaby's very own "Ask an Expert" regular contributor, Simona Montanari, Ph. D., is living proof that one mom, equipped with the right tools and knowledge, can convince a school to add a language immersion program. Montanari is credited with being instrumental in bringing the Italian program to Franklin Elementary Magnet School in Glendale, California.

153

Motivated by the fact that her eldest daughter had one more year before starting kindergarten, Montanari knew she needed to start looking at her options.

"I feel that if you are not educated in the language, you don't truly become bilingual and biliterate," she explains.

Montanari, an assistant professor of Child and Family Studies at California State University in Los Angeles, has two trilingual daughters whose first language is Italian. When she found out about the programs already available in Spanish, Korean and German in Glendale Unified she arranged a meeting with district officials to discuss the possibility of adding an Italian dual immersion program. She was basically told that if she could find enough parents interested in it, they would consider it.

Montanari used all her available resources and was successful at launching the Italian program, which is now thriving. She recognizes she had a clear advantage because she's an expert in the topic of bilingualism, but you too can gather as much information as possible to make your case and follow these five tips:

1. Approach the school district with passion and commitment. Show them you know what you are talking about. Gather as much research as you can.
2. Recruit as many people as possible who support your goal.
3. Enlist the help of a well-known community leader, a school board member or anyone influential who will advocate with you.
4. Find bilingualism experts who are willing to support you and invite them to talk to those with the power to make a decision.
5. Offer something extra. If there's a school in the district with declining enrollment, prove how a program of this nature could turn things around.

The future of bilingual education and the role dual language programs play in it is still being mapped out. What is clear is that we, the parents, are leading the movement by constantly educating ourselves about the benefits of raising a new multilingual and multicultural generation. Let's continue to tread ahead by being language teachers and advocates for our kids as soon as they are born, and let's make our states accountable for allowing our children the right to continue growing as bilinguals the day they enter the public education system.

Between Two Worlds: Identity vs. Assimilation

ROXANA A. SOTO

***

I USED TO WORSHIP MY DAD UNTIL THE DAY HE ANNOUNCED WE WERE moving to *Estados Unidos*. I can't really say I remember the actual day this happened. Back when I was a child, kids weren't privy to their parents' decisions, nor were they asked for their opinions. Either way, what I do remember is that a few months before the drastic change in our lives, things at home were no longer the same.

My mom, dad and older sister traveled to the United States in March 1987. I remember they were going to Washington D.C. where my dad had to attend a series of business meetings that would decide his future in the company for which he worked. My little brother, *Socks*, our cocker spaniel, and I stayed behind in Lima with my *abuelita*. My dad and my sister never came back to Peru. Apparently, my dad was able to get a transfer to Miami, making one of his and my mom's long-time dreams finally come true: going back to live in the United States where my sister had been born eighteen years before.

Truth is that I don't remember how they broke the news to my brother and I, either. They must have known for a while that this was in the works. I mean, things in Peru were getting pretty dangerous, in terms of the government and Sendero Luminoso's terrorist attacks. We grew accustomed to the constant blackouts, curfews and kidnappings but, little by little, the bombs were starting to explode closer to the city, closer to us all. But I'd be lying if I said that any of this fazed me. I was a teenager. I had just turned fourteen. I loved the school I attended. My sister had just graduated from there and it also happened to be my mom and her sisters' alma mater. I got to hang out with my favorite cousin almost every weekend and we spent our entire summers at the beach, in El Silencio, the one place I associate most with my happy childhood days. I also loved the *parrilladas* my father used to host for our extended family every Sunday. It was a tradition and the one time of the week that we'd all get together without fail. It was heaven.

What I do remember very clearly was crying a lot when I found out we were moving again. I hated the idea of having to leave everything behind and move to a foreign country, which I only knew from my gringo teen magazines (I was in love with Tom Cruise and the kid from *Growing Pains!*).

For once, I just wanted to stay put.

It seems crazy, even to me, that someone who had spent most of her short life away from her homeland had trouble adjusting to another move. But maybe it's for that same reason that I hated the fact that we were picking up and starting all over once again. Maybe it was my age. Maybe it was the idea that I'd have to speak English all day long. Maybe I didn't want to be far away from my extended family once again. Maybe I just wanted to feel like I finally belonged. I don't know, but the fact is that when we finally got to Miami, my dad had fallen pretty far off the pedestal.

Although it felt like an eternity at the time, I eventually did find my way in my new country. As I mentioned in the introduction to this book, because I rejected all things American when I first moved here, I made sure to only make friends with other recent immigrants, whose first language was Spanish, or those who'd been here a bit longer but were fully bilingual. In retrospect, I realize that I consciously stayed away from kids who considered themselves Latino, but didn't speak Spanish or were too many generations removed from the immigrant experience, like many of the Cuban-Americans in Miami, for example. And so I ended up befriending kids from Nicaragua, Colombia, Peru and Venezuela. In doing so, I think I felt like I belonged, like these people understood me. After all, we were all going through the same exact thing: struggling with who we were as dictated by where we came from while we tried to assimilate to our new reality.

Little by little, I adjusted. I went to school, I got a part-time job, I had a boyfriend. We went to parties, to the movies and spent tons of weekends cruising Coconut Grove, just like almost every other American teenager I knew back then in South Florida. But we also spent a lot of time with each other's families, like any good Peruvian girl and Nicaraguan boy would do. And while I looked for every single opportunity to speak Spanish on a daily basis, the one class I excelled at in school was English. In fact, I was the editor-in-chief of my school's newspaper, and I had an internship at *The Miami Herald* my senior year in high school. Clearly, I had assimilated well.

I'm not really sure if in my case it was an actual conscious decision, but I think there comes a time in every immigrant's life when there's a need for us to reconcile both our cultures. At some point, we need to come to terms with our new lives and, I dare say, go as far as forging a new identity born out of the unique experience of constantly having to straddle two completely different worlds.

THE ART OF MESHING TWO CULTURES

A friend of mine once described what it means to be Latina in the United States in the following way: "It's like we have two personalities." And I couldn't agree more. From the way our names are pronounced (Roxanne instead of Roxana) to the way we greet an individual (handshake instead of a kiss), if you're bicultural you know the way you act depends on the situation and the people involved. The way I see it, we're also very lucky because we can take the best from both worlds.

But sometimes it can also mean feeling like you don't really belong anywhere. "*No soy ni de aquí ni de allá,*" is a common sentiment among immigrants who feel like they're neither from here nor there. At times, I have felt just like that myself. For example, I never lived in Peru as an adult and even though I've traveled back home regularly throughout the years I've lived in the United States, I still feel very lost whenever there's talk of politics or the economy. While I try to keep up with major news coming out of my home country, the reality is that I don't live there so I'm not affected by what happens there on a daily basis. On the other hand, I sometimes have a hard time relating on a deeper level with people in the United States—even Latinos—who've never experienced what it's like to live in a Latin American country, who don't speak Spanish and who don't understand that what sounds like screaming to them is usually just two people discussing something they're passionate about.

That's probably why I feel more comfortable when I'm around people with the same cultural baggage as me. One of my favorite bilingualism experts, Professor François Grosjean, put it this way (and I immediately felt he was writing about me):

> "Biculturals often say that life is easier when they are with other people with the same bicultural background as them. They can relax and not have to worry about getting things right all the time. They often state that their good

friends (or dream partners) are people like them, with whom they can be totally at ease about their languages and their culture."

This is a big reason why I was originally attracted to my husband and why my really good friends are people like Ana. I feel we understand each other much better because we share similar backgrounds. So, while I can function perfectly well among a group of monocultural and monolingual (whether English-only or Spanish-only) individuals, I always feel much more at ease, like I can be my real self, when I'm surrounded by others who speak both my languages and live in both my cultures (American and Latino). To me it not only means that I can code-switch—or use Spanglish—but also that we can talk about the latest *chisme* in the world of Latino entertainment as well as which team we're rooting for in the Super Bowl.

Whenever my husband and I get together with other bilingual and bicultural friends, we somehow end up talking about how different things are in our home countries. One favorite subject, for example, is the noise level in the streets of Latin America. *La bulla.* While big U.S. cities like New York, Chicago, L.A. and Miami can be extremely loud, nothing really compares to the incessant horns being honked, the uncontrolled screaming of public transportation drivers and the overall noise made by cars so old that it's a miracle they're still circulating.

"I don't know what my car's horn sounds like," a Venezuelan friend of mine once told me. And I almost died laughing because I knew exactly what he was talking about. In most U.S. cities, like Denver where I currently live, honking your horn seems so out of place that you actually turn around to see what prompted it whenever it does happen.

Traffic is another subject that usually comes up when I'm among bicultural friends. Truth is that you haven't experienced traffic until you've been to Latin America. If you've ever traveled to Mexico City, I don't need to explain what I'm talking about. An aunt of mine who has lived there for more than forty years is infamous for her horrific driving record, which includes going backwards on the highway after realizing she missed her exit!

Although Lima is small in comparison to Mexico's capital, one of the things I dread the most is its traffic. The initial shock is always the hardest to get over. I often joke about how all I do from the moment I get in the car at the airport until I get to my grandmother's apartment is pray that we make it alive. I cannot fathom, not even for one second, getting behind the wheel of a car while I'm vacationing there. And it's one of the things I'm grateful to leave behind once we come back to the United States.

These are examples of things I don't miss at all about living in Peru, but the list of those I do miss seems to get longer the older I get.

The taste of the fruit, for example, is on that list. I'll never understand why fruit never tastes the same in the United States. Some claim that if you buy organic, you can get pretty close, but I'm not completely convinced. Not to mention that some fruits, like my favorite *granadilla,* are impossible to find here. That's why I go on a fruit-eating frenzy whenever I travel to Latin America. Back home in Peru, my family is well aware of my addiction to *granadillas* and will have several kilos waiting for me to eat as soon as I land. In fact, there's a running joke in my family that I once missed my flight back to the United

States because I was stuffing myself with *granadillas*. It's not completely true, of course, but it's not completely false either!

Another thing I miss and that I haven't been able to get over and adapt to even after twenty-five years in the United States is meal times—especially when it comes to dinner. Peruvians eat dinner late and it's usually a heavy meal. Even though I'm fully aware that it's not healthy to eat a lot so late at night, I can't deal with the idea of eating dinner by 6 p.m. I no longer have dinner as late as we used to when I lived in Peru, but rare is the day I'll eat my last meal before 8 p.m. (By the way, this only applies to my children on the weekends, since at least one of them is already in school.)

Of course this cultural tug of war goes both ways, and my adopted country has not left me untouched. Although there are tons of things I miss about Peru, there are at least two major aspects of how life is conducted there that I'm always grateful I don't have to deal with in the United States. The first one is that—and I hate to say it—Peru is the most racist and classist country I have ever lived in. I can't really speak for other countries in Latin America, but I suspect many of them are the same way. In my home country, it's not unusual to be asked what your surname is and what school you went to, for example, as a way to determine your social status. There's a humongous gap between the haves and the have-nots and, although things are slowly starting to change, the whole last name thing still doesn't make sense to me because that would imply that everybody knows everybody. But I guess that's the whole point. If your last name is not well known, then that could actually mean that you don't belong to the same social stratosphere as the person asking the question. In terms of the question about which school you attended, that has a lot to do with the fact that most middle and upper class families wouldn't dare send their children to a public school. Private schools, then, become the only option and pretty much everybody knows what tuition is like for the top schools in the city. It's not unusual for parents to pay an average of $800 a month for these private schools, so you can easily imagine what a family of five would pay in tuition alone. Either way, I always thought this was ludicrous, as my sister and I went to one of the most prestigious schools in Lima and yet my family definitely didn't belong to the upper class. Our school's tuition just happened to be a part of my dad's employment contract.

The other thing I don't miss at all is how everyone's always worried about "*el qué dirán*" or what others might say or think of you and your family based on what you say, what you do, how you dress or how you act under any particular circumstance. Here's a prime example: one of my dear cousins had started seeing a guy several years after she got divorced from her first husband. Several months into their relationship, they found out she was pregnant, which only meant they would have to get married a bit earlier than anticipated. My cousin's dad, my uncle, was devastated. He couldn't believe my cousin had done something like this to him and was horrified about what others would say. In case you're wondering, my cousin was thirty years old at the time and, like I already stated, had already been married! These are the type of things that I will never ever understand nor do I ever want to have to explain them to my children.

Whenever I bring these subjects up with my family back home, those who've never left Peru don't seem to know what I'm talking about. But the same thing happens when I talk about this with people who have never left the United States. I guess you have to experience both cultures to be able to make such comparisons.

All of this is only a tiny glimpse into what it's like to live between two worlds, two cultures, two languages and two sets of rules in terms of social behavior. I bring all this up because, as an immigrant who has experienced life in both worlds, I often wonder if my children—who are second-generation Latinos—will feel the same way. The short answer is: probably not. Unless my husband and I one day accomplish our dream of temporarily moving back to Latin America to solidify our children's Spanish and immerse them in our culture. In the meantime, it's up to us—my husband and I—to instill in them a love for their heritage culture while remembering to give the same importance to the culture of the United States, the country of their birth. A delicate balance that should be approached with care and respect.

My daughter, Vanessa, is obsessed with maps and flags. She likes geography, just like her mom. She's very familiar with the U.S. and Colorado flags and we've been teaching her to recognize the Puerto Rican and Peruvian flags. I'm pretty sure our nanny has taught her about the Mexican flag, too. Sometimes, when she spots an American flag, she'll yell: "*Mira, ¡nuestra bandera!*" or "*Mira, ¡la bandera de nuestro país!*" (meaning: "Look, our flag!") I quickly, but gently, correct her by telling her that that's her flag and that mine is red, white and red. I know she's still too little to understand what it all means and so I try to follow a comment like that with a more detailed explanation. For example, we have a huge map hanging on the wall of my home office and I use it, among other things, to teach Vanessa and Santiago where they were born (Colorado), where their older brother was born (Florida), where their dad was born (Puerto Rico) and where I was born (Peru).

Although there are lots of aspects of American culture that I don't necessarily agree with, I want to make sure my children love and respect the country of their birth as much as their heritage culture. Thus, I try to avoid making comments that could sound negative and concentrate on the positives. That's why I'm already working on passing on my passion for American football, a sport I learned to love while in college in Florida. It's also why I make sure we celebrate Thanksgiving every year, even though it's not a tradition that's close to my heart.

Some things, however, I refuse to do. So I've never served my children mac and cheese, and I won't allow them to get up from the table unless *la sobremesa* is over nor will I ever leave the television on while we're eating—which goes to show the power my Latino cultural background has on the way I'm parenting my children.

Lately, though, there's one aspect of this cultural tug of war involving identity and assimilation that has been bugging me more than ever before.

ON BECOMING AN AMERICAN (OR NOT)

I'm not a U.S. citizen. I'm the only one in my family who isn't.

My husband was born in Puerto Rico—a colony of the United States—and both our children were born in Colorado. So they're all American by birth. My older sister was born here when my father was a student in Florida. Although they went back to Peru when she was not even one, when we came back to the States many years later, my parents obtained their legal permanent residency through her. Once they were residents, they petitioned for my little brother and I. After spending the five years as legal permanent residents required by law, they all became naturalized citizens. I, on the other hand, opted against it.

The reasons behind that decision have been the source of many an argument between my husband and I and—when he was alive—between my father and I. It's not really a subject I like to discuss—especially during these contentious political times full of anti-immigrant backlash, but I figured that sharing my personal struggle with this subject could resonate with other people out there who feel the same way.

But first, some background.

After moving to the United States in 1987, I wasn't able to go back to Peru for six years. Part of it was cost related and part of it had to do with the immigration regulations attached to my father's work visa. When our permanent residency papers finally came through in 1993, it required both my little brother and I to go back to Peru to finalize the process. I was twenty years old at the time, a sophomore at the University of Florida, and to this day, I remember how euphoric I was to finally go home. I'd left a child and I was going back a woman.

Although at that point I'd gotten over a lot of the resentment and anger I had when we first moved to Miami when I was fourteen, going back home after such a long time opened up a lot of wounds. Seeing my cousin for the first time in six years was bittersweet. We couldn't stop hugging and kissing each other, and we spent countless sleepless nights trying to catch up on the past six years of our lives. Doing so, in turn, reminded me how much I missed out on and how difficult moving and adapting to a whole new life in the United States had really been. Even today, writing about it brings unexpected tears to my eyes because I can't help but feel like I was robbed of something very precious: a chance to grow up surrounded by the unconditional love of the people who've known me since the moment I was born. The kind of people who see pictures of my daughter Vanessa and immediately recognize a five-year-old me back in the 1970s. Most people who didn't know me then think she looks exactly like her father. They see none of me in her.

Today, I know in my heart of hearts that my dad made the right decision accepting a job transfer to Miami. Today, I can't deny that the opportunities we were presented with here were second to none. I mean, where else would an eighteen-year-old journalism student be given an opportunity to get published on a regular basis in a major newspaper only four years after immigrating? So with time, I came to be happy—and grateful—for the life I had carved for myself in the United States, but I never felt completely whole. Something was always missing. For years, I couldn't help but wonder what my life would've been like if I hadn't been separated from my extended family, my friends, my culture, my school, my food.

Once I became a legal permanent resident and was able to go back home as often as possible, I took every opportunity to do so. As a senior in college, I once made the trip back home just for the weekend to surprise a very close grade school friend of mine at her wedding. Needless to say, she was speechless when she saw me, and we talk about it to this day. The trip was not cheap—especially for a broke college student—and I missed a major class assignment because of it, but it was my way of clinging to anything that would allow me to feel like I was still a part of my beloved *patria* and an important part of my life that I had left behind as a child almost a decade before.

Years later, I was offered a dream job as a television producer for Univision's weekly newsmagazine show, *Aquí y Ahora*, where I was able to combine my love of journalism with my love of travel—especially back to my home country. For more than four years, every time there was a major news story in Peru, I volunteered to work on it as soon as it broke. As usual, I would work like a fiend, but I was almost always able to have dinner with my family on a nightly basis and I'd make sure to extend my trips through the weekend so I could spend more time with them. Somehow, I had found a way to continue living with one foot in each world. *La historia de todos los inmigrantes.*

When my time at Univision came to an end, I was most sad about losing the recurring opportunities to go back home. I continued going there on vacation, but there was no way I could afford traveling there as often as I had for work. Eventually, I accepted that no matter how much I traveled back to Peru, my real life was in the United States. This realization, in turn, made me want to hold on to my cultural identity even more. So, when the time came for my brother and I to become naturalized citizens, I kept on delaying the process. My dad was constantly after me to finish the paperwork and I always had one excuse after another: the application was too long; I was too busy with work; I had to report all the times I'd left the country since we'd arrived which, considering my job, seemed completely daunting; etc., etc. My father was so intent on me becoming a citizen that he offered to fill out the application for me. I turned him down, reminding him I was old enough to take care of it myself.

But my father was not stupid and, as someone who loved the country of his birth like no other, he knew very well that my reasons for not completing the application had nothing to do with time and everything to do with principle. In essence, how can I agree to become a citizen of the United States when my heart and soul are so deeply Peruvian? To a lot of people, one thing has nothing to do with the other. They see it all in terms of practicalities. Just because you become an

American citizen doesn't mean you're no longer Peruvian, they tell me. Plus, both countries allow you to have dual citizenship, they add. Still, it just doesn't feel right.

It's not that I have anything at all against my adopted country. My children wouldn't have been born here if that were the case. It's just something that is really hard to explain, but I will try—even though I'll probably get lynched in the process. I like the United States, but I love Peru. I'll stand up as a sign of respect when someone recites the pledge of allegiance or sings the national anthem, but I won't follow their lead. The only anthem I know by heart and can sing at a moment's notice is the Peruvian one. I think the Stars and Stripes is beautiful, but I only get butterflies in my stomach when I see the red, white and red flag of my birth country. I could go on and on, but I think this will have to suffice.

Even so, three things have made me analyze my decision not to become a U.S. citizen a bit deeper lately.

The first one has to do with the fact that at thirty-nine years old, I have never voted, which is very weird because I've always been interested in politics and I am, after all, a journalist. Yet, I've never partaken in what I consider one of the most vital parts of belonging to a democracy. I've never voted not because I didn't want to, but because I can't—although my husband would beg to differ. Let's see, if we were to get technical, I could actually vote—in Peruvian elections, that is. Yet even though I've covered Peru's elections a couple of times as a journalist, the reality is that I have absolutely no connection to my home country's politics.

My husband, however, disagrees about me not being able to vote because I could've become an American citizen fourteen years ago—meaning I've missed almost four presidential elections and twice as many at the state and city level.

I must admit I was jealous of my husband when he voted for Obama in 2008. There was so much presidential buzz going on back then. It was an exciting time for sure! Plus, he actually got to meet Obama during a one-on-one interview he taped for Univision and we both got to cover the Democratic National Convention in Denver.

A few days prior to a recent election, my husband told me he was never going to vote again. "It's all the same," he lamented. "They're all the same." He, like many others who voted for Obama, was disillusioned. He felt too many promises were broken. "It's hard fixing something that's so broken," I told him. But he didn't care. Then he covered an event in which a local Latina activist talked about the power of just one vote and he came back a changed man.

"I don't know what I was thinking," he confessed. "If we all think the way I was thinking, then nothing will ever change."

After he voted, he came home feeling pretty empowered. I hate not knowing what that feels like. I used to be a lot more vocal about my political views, but I've toned down a bit because the truth is that I shouldn't be able to complain about something I don't agree with if I'm not able to vote to try to change it, no?

The second reason I'm rethinking my citizenship status has to do with convenience. Having an American passport is an extremely powerful tool, but for more reasons than just the obvious. Even with all the negative coverage the United States has gotten from the international media in years past, having an American passport still easily opens up the world to those who hold one. I, on the other hand, have always had to go through the painstaking process of getting a tourist visa— which can not only be very expensive, but also daunting and time consuming—whenever I want to travel pretty much anywhere other than the country of my birth.

For someone who loves to travel as much as I do, going through the naturalization process and obtaining an American passport would seem like the most logical thing to do.

Last, but definitely not least, I am now a mother, no longer capable of making decisions without worrying about the collateral effects. While I dream of one day going back to live in Peru, even temporarily, the truth is that I've been in this country for close to three decades. I became a professional journalist, a wife and a mother right here where my children were born. And, at least for the time being, I don't really think we're going anywhere. Plus, given the current anti-immigrant sentiment in this country, I truly think it would behoove me to leave my patriotic ideals behind and become an American citizen once and for all.

Whenever I think about that actually happening though, I wonder how I will feel the day of the naturalization ceremony. I know that for so many people—my parents included—this is an extremely important day, one full of emotions and gratitude. I must confess, though, that I don't really understand or, better yet, I can't relate to those comments. I know this opens up the doors to lots of criticism, and I'm ready to take it. I probably deserve it, but I can't help my feelings.

ANA SPEAKS OUT ABOUT HER HUSBAND'S STRUGGLE WITH BECOMING A U.S. CITIZEN

I CAN IMAGINE ONE OF THE MOST CONTROVERSIAL SUBJECTS IN THIS CHAPTER will be Roxana's confession that she has had a very hard time deciding to become a U.S. citizen. I'm sure this will cause a lot of judgement from so many who could only wish to be in her position and would never pass up such an amazing opportunity. I do understand where she's coming from, yet can't completely grasp why not just deal with it *y ya!*

The thing is Roxana is not the only person I know and care for that feels this way. The other is my own husband.

My husband and I met while I was living in Mexico. He had just come back from living in Miami for work, right after he graduated from the Savannah College of Art and Design where he had been recruited to attend on a full soccer scholarship. Those five years between Georgia and Florida had been the extent of his life in the United States. Born and raised in Mexico, he studied at the American School in Mexico City. Even though he's half European (Dutch father) and half Mexican (mother), he's 100% *Chilango* (a term to describe people from Mexico City).

When he and I met we had no plans to live in the United States. After five years living in Mexico, I was already feeling very Mexican and so connected to the rich heritage and traditions of the country which had adopted me. But then one day, out of the blue, BOTH of us got job offers to move to Los Angeles to work for mun2, a cable channel aimed at Latino youth, which is owned by NBC Universal.

Since we were already married and I am a U.S. citizen by birth, it was not difficult to get his work visa so we could move to the United States. This was an opportunity two TV people could not pass up. This was in 2006. Soon after, we became parents to a little girl who already had a U.S. and a Dutch passport by the time she was one.

My husband has officially been toting his green card for seven years now. He's more than eligible to become a U.S. citizen, but he's just not ready. His reasons are pretty much the same as Roxana's. He basically feels he's not American enough to call himself a citizen. I find this difficult to swallow because there has to come a time when you fully accept that it's okay to belong to and fully embrace two cultures. I constantly remind him that his daughter will not understand his reasons because this is her *casa*. How will he one day explain to her that he cannot vote to protect her rights because his soul belongs to another country? How will our girl grasp that when she doesn't have the same connection we have to Mexico? If she remains in this country, she will never truly understand what assimilation means and how her father's personal identity is linked to his home country and the nuances of the way of life he grew up with.

In that case, our daughter might have an easier time relating to my life experience of being completely assimilated, identified and at ease between two cultures. At least I hope that's what we manage to give her.

Like Roxana, my husband has come to terms with his life in California, a life he loves and can't imagine leaving right now. He's grateful for the many opportunities we've had, mostly due to our bilingual and bicultural upbringings, and he now has enough invested in the country's politics to feel the need to have his vote counted. Assimilation in day-to-day life has been easy for him—a white, green-eyed Mexican—but his identity as a *Chilango* will be forever ingrained in him.

FEELING DISCRIMINATION

Despite my non-citizen status, I have always felt very welcomed in my adopted country.

I'm either blind or extremely oblivious, but I don't think I can say I've ever experienced discrimination in the United States. Or, it could also be that it would take a lot for me to feel discriminated against. In other words, I've never felt like a few idiotic and ignorant phrases directed specifically at me or at Latinos in general classify as discrimination. Don't get me wrong, though, I'm by no means saying that Latinos are not discriminated. I know for a fact they are. I'm a journalist, and I've covered cases of blatant discrimination on a regular basis. But to say that I've felt it myself would be a lie. Maybe I should consider myself lucky or maybe luck has nothing to do with it.

One thing I do know is that living in Miami makes it kind of difficult to feel discriminated against because Latinos own and rule South Florida. So much so that if you don't speak Spanish in Miami, you can't really survive. English is absolutely unnecessary. Okay, that might be a stretch, but it surely felt like during that the nineteen years I lived there. Yet, to say that it's because I lived in Miami that I've never felt discrimination would be incorrect. After all, I went to college in Gainesville in northern Florida a stone's throw away from states like Georgia and Alabama, where Latinos definitely do not rule the land. And I now live in Denver, Colorado—not exactly a Latino haven either.

We've been in Denver since 2006, a few weeks before Vanessa was born, and we live in the suburbs to the south where Latinos are barely on the radar. Yet, I've never ever felt out of place or singled out, even when I only speak Spanish to my children regardless of where we are—which I'm sure doesn't make some people here happy. If that's the case, though, they've never let it be known. In fact, the opposite is true. At both my kids' schools, for example, every time I've had to explain to their teachers that their first language is Spanish, I've never been met with any resistance, rejection or outright criticism. On the contrary, I've been praised and they have been applauded. In our picture perfect neighborhood, we've never felt like we're being treated differently because we are Latino. We love where we live and are grateful for our neighbors' kindness, which has ranged from helping us with our kids by babysitting to shoveling our driveway after a snowstorm without being asked. Again, maybe I just got lucky.

MIAMI TO DENVER:
THE DEFINITION OF CULTURE SHOCK

That's not to say, however, that moving from Miami to Denver was not a complete shock to our systems in the beginning. My husband and I often joke that after living for twenty years in South Florida, coming to Colorado felt like we'd finally arrived to the United States! I know it sounds like an exaggeration, but that's what happens when, all of a sudden, you're surrounded by white people who only speak English, are courteous and respect the traffic signals.

Joking aside, moving to Denver meant serious culture shock. First of all, even though the Mexican community here is large and visible, my Caribbean husband and I didn't really identify with it—especially because the large majority of Mexican immigrants here are either from northern Mexico or they're Chicanos, an ethnic group we'd never encountered before. So from their music—*corridos* and *norteñas*—to their food—burritos and green chile stew—my husband and I have been introduced to a completely different type of Latino culture since we moved to Colorado.

And then, of course, there is the fact that Latinos make up only 32% of the population in Denver, whereas they make up 70% of Miami's population, according to the 2010 U.S. Census. We're certainly a minority here, albeit a growing one. In our neighborhood in the suburbs, which I've already mentioned we love, we are the only Latino family. Okay, that's a bit of a lie because, as luck would have it, my next-door neighbor is actually Colombian! But the truth is she left her homeland many decades ago to settle in Ohio and is really more American than anything else. Although, we do speak Spanish whenever we see each other, which I love because my kids have been able to communicate with her since before they learned how to speak English.

In school, my children had always been the only dark haired, dark eyed ones in a sea of blue eyed blondes, until last year when Vanessa entered kindergarten. There were two Mexican boys in her class. One was a recent immigrant, while the other one, from his knowledge of English, had obviously been here much longer. I was surprised to see them, but I was mostly elated because Vanessa would have more people with whom to speak Spanish. In fact, I was extremely proud to see my bilingual daughter become an intermediary of sorts between the non-English-speaking boy and his English-only school community. As expected, it didn't take him long to learn English. Within a few months, he was speaking it fluently and without an accent, but he and my daughter still communicated in Spanish, their first language.

Examples like these, however, are few and far between. Our daily lives in the suburbs of Denver unfold surrounded exclusively by English and the American culture. I must say that once we realized and accepted our new reality, adjusting became a bit easier. Still, it's a work in progress and there are some aspects which we might never get used to or at least we haven't just yet.

Because Latinos have less of an influence in Denver, our entertainment choices, for example, are also limited. I'll never forget the shock on my husband's face when he heard salsa superstar Oscar d'Leon was coming to town to play at a local nightclub, which was not even in Denver. Used to the popularity of salsa not only in his native Puerto Rico, but also in Miami, this was hard to fathom for my husband. I guess we should just count our blessings because being part of a much smaller Latino community has allowed us to watch performers like Juanes and Maná in more intimate settings.

But, by far, lack of options in terms of food and food products has been one of the most difficult things to adjust to for both my husband and me. Coming from Miami where we could virtually find food from anywhere in Latin America, we've had to content ourselves with the handful of Latino restaurants that cater to anyone other than Mexicans. When it comes to the products we need to cook specific Peruvian or Puerto Rican dishes, we've had to rely on the internet or beg a kind traveling soul to bring them back from Miami, Puerto Rico or Peru. On occasion, we've lucked out and found some of these food products at so-called Hispanic markets and we've had no doubts about paying their hefty, obviously marked-up prices—like I did when I found *ají amarillo*, a staple of Peruvian cuisine, earlier this year.

Speaking of Hispanic products, I hate when I go to the supermarket and head to the "Hispanic Food" section only to find a few shelves full of Mexican items! I should note here that I have nothing against Mexicans—half of my family on my mom's side is from that majestic country—but come on, why don't they just call it what it is, the "Mexican Food" section? I guess I should be grateful that there's even a section for these items in the highly white suburbs we call home. I don't expect for Peruvian items to make it to the shelves of any American supermarket in this area, although that would undoubtedly be grandiose. The only Hispanic market in the area closed a couple of years ago and now I have to make a concerted effort to go to the other ones far, far away from home so I can get some overpriced *aceitunas de botija, ají amarillo* or Goya items for my husband to cook some Puerto Rican food.

So while I'm thankful that my local supermarkets are making an effort, what I do have a problem with is the erroneous assumption that Hispanic equals Mexican. That's just like when I'm asked if I speak Mexican instead of Spanish. None of the stuff on the shelves of the "Hispanic Food" section at the local market would be useful in my kitchen—except for maybe the chocolate bars to make *chocolate caliente,* even though they're not the Abuelita brand I really like. Every time I go into a new—meaning I've never been there—supermarket near my house or office, I want to believe that maybe this one got it right. But no, every single time I'm disappointed by the same old Mexican items.

I know ignorance is what makes people think that all Latinos are the same, but that doesn't make it any better. Hopefully, as the Latino population continues to grow and expand throughout the country, we'll be able to deconstruct at least the most prevalent of the abundant stereotypes surrounding our culture. Eventually, others will realize that being Latino doesn't necessarily mean you eat tacos or hot sauces, dance salsa, are sex-crazed or even that you speak Spanish. After all, as we've already seen, only a measly 38% of third generation Latinos speak the mother tongue proficiently.

THE TRUTH ABOUT SPANISH, ENGLISH AND SPANGLISH

IT HAS LONG BEEN BELIEVED THAT FOR IMMIGRANTS TO BECOME "AMERICAN" they must "disconnect from the old and connect to the new" as did those who came before them. In other words, they must assimilate to the culture of their new home. One of the first and most important ways of assimilating, many will say, is by learning the English language which, according to anti-immigration supporters, today's Latino immigrants refuse to do. But a quick look at the available data shows this belief is unfounded.

According to a series of surveys by the Pew Hispanic Center, while only 23% of first generation Latinos report being able to speak English very well, the number almost quadruples when it comes to their U.S. born adult children (80% say they speak English very well). By the third generation, the figure rises to 94%, helping to explain why so many people with Spanish or Latino surnames like Martinez, Gonzalez or Vigil don't speak a word of Spanish—especially in the Southwest.

In states like Texas, Arizona, New Mexico and Colorado, it is not uncommon to hear stories like this one from third generation Latinos: "My parents were among the generation that was whipped for speaking Spanish in school, and as a result, my grandparents stopped speaking to them in Spanish so they could learn English better."

In these same states, signs excluding Mexicans and dogs from establishments were not hard to find. Speaking Spanish was viewed not only as a handicap, but also as a justification for discrimination.

Things have obviously changed, but Spanish continues to lack the prestige other foreign languages enjoy. Thus, I'd still be hard-pressed to find a Latino immigrant parent who's not interested in their children learning English. In fact, there's an erroneous belief among many first generation Latino immigrant parents (as well as educators) that in order for their children to learn English they should not be exposed to Spanish at all. During an interview I conducted with the director of a full immersion dual language school which opened in Denver in 2011, I was surprised to find out that many first generation parents were genuinely not interested in such a program because their biggest desire was for their children to learn English—not Spanish—so they could have the kind of success that eluded their parents due to their lack of English skills.

It's not surprising then that Spanish is watered down by the time we get to the third generation. This is how it happens: first generation immigrants usually learn enough English to survive but conduct themselves mostly in Spanish in their daily lives. Their children—or the second generation (whether they were born here or came when they were very young)—maintain their Spanish (mostly spoken only), but conduct themselves mainly in English in their daily lives. Their grandchildren—or the third generation—speak only English.

This trend is supported by another set of data also released by The Pew Hispanic Center. According to one of their studies, only 38% of third generation Latinos are proficient in Spanish. That's a huge drop when compared to second generation Latinos, 79% of whom are proficient in the language of their ancestors. Contrary to popular belief, these numbers follow a similar pattern in terms of what has happened historically with immigrants and their heritage languages.

But there's a very explicit danger in assimilating. "If we're not connected to our past, to our ancestors, we lose our identity, we lose our sense of self," a professor of Chicano Studies once told me. I agree wholeheartedly and that's why I won't get tired of saying that, to me, raising Vanessa and Santiago to be bilingual has a lot more to do with cultural heritage than with future job opportunities. It's an added blessing that being bilingual brings about so many intellectual benefits, but the connection to our Latino roots through our heritage language is of much more importance to me and Ana. In the end, that's the reason why SpanglishBaby even exists. And, obviously, we're not alone. In fact, the threat of losing the heritage language what has given rise to the popularity of our blog, as lots of Latino parents—many of whom are third generation—are looking for ways to hang on to their ancestor's culture at any cost.

ON HAVING AN ACCENT

Another thing that became very clear once we moved to Denver was my accent when I speak English. I mean, I've always known I had one, but it certainly was not an issue in Miami, where speaking English with a Spanish accent is "normal." But in Denver, my accent apparently stands out, as I found out one day at my neighborhood's craft store. I was explaining the materials I was looking for to an employee at the framing department. I think she was frustrated because the store didn't carry one of the products I was looking for, so she ended up asking me if I'd rather talk to someone in Spanish. I thanked her for the offer, but declined and went on to finish the rest of my shopping... mad.

Coincidentally, that same week, I had gotten a similar offer from someone at a local government agency. We had been on the phone for at least ten minutes, and I just needed one more piece of information before we were done. All of a sudden, she blatantly, albeit politely, told me she could detect an accent when I spoke and asked if I'd rather talk to someone in Spanish. I incredulously declined her offer by explaining politely that I was bilingual. We went on with the conversation, but I was pretty bitter by the time we hung up. My husband couldn't understand why I was angry, but I guess it really bothered me that, twice in one week, someone thought I didn't know how to speak English because I have a Spanish accent when I speak it.

The subject of accents is both tricky and touchy. I've always felt like I don't really care if I have one, but maybe I've just learned to accept it since I'm fully aware that not speaking English is not an option. Although if I never had to do it in front of a large group of people, I'd be really happy. Apparently, I'm not alone. One day, my husband was prepping for a presentation for one of the classes he takes at the local university when I asked him how he felt about public speaking. He said it had gotten much easier with time, but that it would be even easier if he didn't have to do it in English, and I was a bit surprised to hear that coming from him.

I've always considered him to be just as bilingual and biliterate as I am. Both of us attended bilingual schools in our home countries and finished our high school education here in the United States. We've always been able to communicate in both languages with the same ease—or so I thought. The thing is I totally understood where he was coming from because I feel exactly the same way, but I'd never really stopped to think about it. In other words, although I hate giving speeches period, I can't deny the dread would be diminished if I could do it in Spanish.

Why? I guess at the end of the day, Spanish is my native language and, although I've gotten over it, I've always been conscious that I have a Spanish accent when I speak English and that there are many words I don't pronounce correctly. In fact, I've been corrected on more than one occasion when I've said the name of my very own blog, SpanglishBaby, in front of a group of parents. The worst part is that, in some cases, the difference in pronunciation is so subtle, I can't really tell I'm not saying something right, but native English speakers can.

This often makes me wonder how it'll be for my children when they get older. Will they have an English accent when they speak Spanish? Will they ever not feel comfortable giving a class presentation in Spanish? Can I prevent that from happening?

This brings up an interesting point about second language acquisition and timing. It should be common knowledge that the younger you learn a second (or third) language, the better chances you have of speaking like a native. So besides the fact that it's easier for children to learn a second language when they're young, one of the most important benefits is that they'll actually learn to speak it with a native or near-native accent. A child's ability to hear different phonetic pronunciations is most acute before the age of three. Countless studies, including one published in the journal *Psychological Science* in 2010, have shown that babies and toddlers are better able to tell the difference among a wider variety of languages than older children and adults.

In her book, *Raising a Bilingual Child,* bilingualism expert, Barbara Zurer Pearson, says that "infants are very good at hearing sound contrasts from birth and are also very good at learning to ignore them from shortly after six months, if they do not continue to hear them in their surroundings." Eventually, children learn to only make the distinctions pertinent to the languages that surround them.

In my case, for example, since I learned my second language after the first one was already in place, I had already learned to ignore any sound contrasts that were not relevant to the Spanish spoken around me. In order to learn the sound differences in English I had to "forget" the ones I already knew in Spanish and start almost from scratch.

In my children's case, however, it seems like the opposite will be true. They are basically exposed to both English and Spanish at the same time. I can already detect, for example, that my daughter will have native accents in both languages as she already makes a distinction even with such simple things as pronouncing her name.

In the end, we all forge our identities out of our own experiences. My children are still too young for me to know for sure how they'll identify themselves later on in their lives. I can only hope that I'm able to give them a real sense of what it means to be an American citizen of Peruvian and Puerto Rican descent. When I look at them now, I like to think we're well on our way. Although fully bilingual, Vanessa already has a preference for books and music in Spanish. Meanwhile, Santiago has already demonstrated his Latino roots more than once in the way his little body instantly sways to the sound of Puerto Rican music and in his indiscriminate preference for the *sofrito*-based food of his father's homeland. While the work always continues, not a day goes by that I don't pray for them to grow up to love and honor their heritage culture and our native language as much as both their parents do.

Raising Bicultural Children in the United States

✳

I HAVE A CONFESSION TO MAKE. I ALWAYS LIKED THE IDEA OF STARTING A blog like SpanglishBaby.com, where Ana and I could share our journeys as we attempt to raise bilingual and bicultural children in the United States, but I never imagined it would become so popular. After almost four years, and as evidenced by the book you're holding in your hands, I can confidently attest to the fact that one of the main reasons why our blog has been so successful is because so many Latino parents feel the same way we do: It is absolutely imperative for us to pass on our heritage to the next generation.

I've always felt like my parents didn't really have to worry about this because, by the time we got to Miami, I had lived embedded in my culture for fourteen years. So it wasn't like they had to teach me all about Peruvian food, music or traditions because I had already experienced them myself. My husband, however, disagrees. He tells me that while I might have already been exposed to my Peruvian culture, my parents did an amazing job making sure it stayed alive after we moved to the United States. From the Peruvian dishes my father cooked daily—yes, my Latino dad did the cooking at home!—to only speaking to my siblings and I in Spanish, even though they were both perfectly bilingual, and everything in between, including nurturing our relationships with the extended family we left behind. Since this was way before the Internet, it involved writing letters (to my *abuelita, mi pa-*

drino, mis tías, mis primos) and the occasional—because of its exorbitant cost—phone call.

I have to be thankful to my parents for always speaking about Peru and our culture with lots of love and respect, for keeping all of our traditions alive and for raising us with the kind of values that no longer seem too popular these days. I grew up in a pretty strict household where children could be seen, but they were not supposed to be heard. My mom was the disciplinarian—mostly because my dad worked all day— and she was one tough lady. I was spanked, for sure, and I have absolutely no issues saying so nor do I feel any type of resentment toward my mother because of it. Let me make it clear: she spanked me, not beat me up. And, I'm sure I deserved it each and every single time. My siblings and I always remember how, when we were in the company of others, it took only one look—*the* look—from my mom to warn us that if we continued with our bad behavior we'd be in huge trouble later. Oh, and *pobre de mí* if I dared to interrupt a conversation between adults. That was a huge no-no. My parents never ever asked us our opinions on anything having to do with our upbringing: from what we were going to eat to what we were going to wear (yet, somehow, I've always been a pretty independent woman). But don't get me wrong, we had the liveliest conversation at the dinner table, the type that opened up our minds and made us inquisitive and informed us about the world around us.

Respect for my elders is a value that is deeply ingrained in me and one of those that don't seem very popular these days. I'm not really sure why this wouldn't be of tremendous importance to any parent, but I think it has to do with the idea that we're all equal and there's no distinction in hierarchy between parents and children. That whole thing about parents being their children's friends is something I'll never understand. I've seen people close to me raise their children that way and then have to deal with the negative consequences later on. I love my mother to death and I've shared lots of personal stuff with her, but that's because she's my mom and I value her views and opinions, not because she's my friend. I think you can have a great parent-child relationship without having to make it into a friendship. I don't think children are looking to have a friendship with their parents, especially in their teenage years when they need guidance and lots of love, more than anything else.

Successfully achieving a healthy parent-child relationship, of course, is another story. Although I wish to raise my children the way my parents raised my siblings and me, I often feel like I'm failing miserably. I can't help but think that it has a lot to do with the intricacies of living between two cultures, two languages and two worlds, influenced by old traditions and values but pressured by new ones.

RAISING A BICULTURAL CHILD

So what does raising a bicultural child in the United States look like?

A couple of recent surveys on Latino parenting practices have shed some light on this question. The first one, released by BabyCenter in 2011, shows how ingrained the Latino culture is in our daily lives regardless of our acculturation level. In their Hispanic Moms Acculturation Study, BabyCenter interviewed 2,479 Hispanic moms—from recent immigrants to native-born English speakers—and 1,472 non-Hispanic moms from both their English and Spanish language sites.

"With one in four babies in this country being Hispanic, and Hispanics representing 55% of the population growth in the United States, this study sheds new light on the behaviors of Latina moms as they go through the acculturation process and integrate elements of American culture with those of their own heritage," BabyCenter explained.

Honestly, according to the results of these studies, I'm not exactly the prototype of the Latina mom and yet I can see some of myself and my family's dynamic in the results. Check out some of the key findings for yourself, and you'll see that many of the practices and values mentioned by these Latina moms are useful tools for helping us keep our culture alive.

The Culture of Food

Meals are an important way for us, Hispanic moms, to connect our families to our *cultura*. 36% of Hispanic moms say dinner is the best time of the day, compared to only 15% of non-Hispanic moms.

This is true in my own household since dinner is the only time—at least during the week—that we can all sit together and share our day with each other. I have extremely fond memories of dinners with my parents as a child. Although they were always an opportunity for our parents to drill table manners into us—"*baja el codo de la mesa*" and "*no hables con la comida en la boca*"—they were also full of interesting conversation about anything and everything. My parents not only allowed us to participate in these conversations, but they also encouraged us to question the world around us, *siempre y cuando* we were respectful of others' views. My children are still too little, but I can't wait until they are old enough for our dinners to be as enjoyable as mine were as a child—at least in terms of the conversation because I surely am not half the cook my dad was.

- Hispanic food—which most of us (not me!) cook from scratch—is part of the daily diet of 41% of Latino families. The numbers change as we acculturate and look for short-cuts to make cooking easier, as in making black beans de lata and not from scratch (yes me!).

I would say food is an extremely important way to make sure we all stay connected to our roots. Eating is one thing Latinos know how to do and not just for nourishment. Meals take on an entirely new meaning when it comes to Latinos. For us, it's all about distinctive flavors, traditions, *la receta de la abuela,* love, family and how many people go for seconds! Right? For all these reasons, food is an excellent way to keep our heritage alive.

If you're like me—more the eating type than the cooking type—and have no idea how to get started cooking traditional dishes, there are tons of really well done blogs, websites and cookbooks designed specifically to help you accomplish this. In my house, neither my husband nor I really know how to cook, but for the sake of passing on our culture to our children, we've made it a point to try to learn how to make at least one or two dishes from our respective home countries. After a couple of questionable attempts, my husband now makes a mean *lechón* and *arroz con habichuelas* which is always devoured by all, especially my son Santiago who seems to have a preference for *comida criolla.* I have never even attempted to make *ceviche*—the expectations I have to live up to are way too high—but

I have mastered a few Peruvian dishes including *lomo saltado, arroz con pollo* and *corvina a la chorrillana.*

If your kids are old enough to help you out in the kitchen, make sure to get them involved. I have yet to meet a child who doesn't like to pretend to be a chef! If your family lives close by or they are planning to visit you, schedule at least one cooking session with them so they can teach you and your kids how to cook a Latino family recipe. When my mother-in-law comes to visit from Puerto Rico, we try to do this and we've found that it's best if we get the whole process on video, that way we can always look back if there's ever a question and she's not available to answer it. We've learned to make her famous *flan de queso* and her delicious *mofongo* this way!

La Familia *First*

- A huge percentage of us, 68% in fact, are likely to eat at least one meal a week with our extended family.

In my own family we don't do this every week, but we try to make it happen as often as possible, and my children love it (I do too!). Of course, I'm lucky to live close to my mother and siblings. If there's one thing I really miss about living in Peru is that every single Sunday was decreed family day, which meant we always got together with our extended family. In the summertime, this usually meant *una parrillada* and while the adults enjoyed their drinks, the children played like there was nothing more important in the world!

• When it comes to aspirations, la familia continues to be número uno, even though professional success is seen as inspiring. The BabyCenter study found that "me" time is not engaging for Hispanic moms.

I'm not really sure about this one because I think that "me" time is hugely important, and I pretty much learned that from my own very Peruvian mother. She always made it clear that she was our mother, but she was also a woman with her own needs and likes and she made time to pursue those. While I don't get as much time for myself as I would like, I'm definitely not the type of mom who puts everyone's needs before hers, like many Latina moms I know, especially the women of my mom's generation.

• We see all celebrations, including our niños' birthday parties, as a chance to connect with our families.

I thought this finding was particularly interesting: "Hispanics include extended family in these celebrations (children's parties) regardless of age." I had never stopped to think about that one, but it's totally true. We invite los abuelos, los tíos, los padrinos and, as the study points out, our parties also last much, much longer than the two and a half hours allotted in the majority of the birthday party invitations my daughter receives. Oh, and we spend more money on our parties than the general population.

It is no secret that Latinos place great importance on tightly knit families, which not only include parents, but also grandparents, uncles, aunts, godparents and cousins. If you're lucky enough to live close to any family at all, make it a point to get together often. Spending time with the family can be an excellent way to keep our *raíces* alive, especially if there are elders involved. Try to engage them in conversations about how life was back in their country of origin, the music they listened to, their favorite dishes—the possibilities are endless.

If you don't have any family near you, then try to make a trip back "home" whenever possible to visit and get a dose of family time Latino-style. If you have children, this will be a great way to immerse them in our culture, our food and our traditions, while teaching them about the importance of family.

Before we even left for our trip back home to Peru in 2011, I started talking to my children about all the family we'd be visiting, the typical Peruvian food we'd be eating, and all the fun stuff we were going to do. My daughter was really excited even before we left because she knew she was going to play with her cousins, whom she adores, even if she only sees them once a year. She was also looking forward to exploring the city where her mother was born and which I proudly showed her.

On Bilingualism

Another survey regarding Latino parenting tendencies in the United States was released in early 2012 as a compilation of answers to several different questions asked by TodoBebé, a leading independent producer of family friendly parenting and entertainment content for the Hispanic market, on their website. One of the most interesting questions had to do with bilingualism.

According to this survey, an overwhelming 97% of respondents agreed it's a good idea to teach your children more than one language. Almost half (49%) said they speak more than one language at home.

I can't deny that I was very pleased with these results because I often worry that a lot of Latino parents are still given the wrong information regarding bilingualism, be it from other family members or from their own child's pediatrician. If so many Latino parents are raising their children to be bilingual, I can only imagine how this will change the face of America and what it will mean for the future of Spanish in the United States. Seeing numbers like these make me really optimistic.

On Discipline

The majority of the moms surveyed (51%) are against spanking as a form of disciplining their children, but 38% say they're for it.

I guess I fall into that minority. As I've already mentioned, I was spanked by my mother growing up, so I don't really think much of it. I've given my children *una que otra nalgada* and I probably will continue to do so when necessary, even though I'm sure that doesn't fly very well with both Latinas and non-Latinas alike.

On Baby Names

- Even though it's a long held tradition in Latin American countries, 69% of respondents said that they don't like children bearing the same name as their parents.

Yet, lots of them—including my own husband—still follow this practice. My stepson bears his father's and grandfather's name, which I never thought was very original, though I understood the tradition behind it. I'm just glad my husband got that out of the way before we had children of our own! I love my dad's name, Miguel, and I did, at one point, think about giving it to my son as a middle name, but everyone in our family has middle names that start with the first letter of the alphabet, so that wouldn't have worked. So much for tradition, right?

While most Latinas don't follow this particular tradition, many of the Latina moms I know do struggle when choosing a baby name in terms of making sure it reflects our culture without being something so out there that mainstream America will have a hard time pronouncing it. The main goal, from what I've been able to gather unscientifically, is for the name to sound the same, or similar, in both English and Spanish. Another example of how we are preparing our children to live between two cultures from the day they are born.

The results of these surveys, as well as the growing popularity of blogs like SpanglishBaby and others with a similar mission, reflect a huge desire among Latino parents to pass along our heritage and language to our children born outside of our culture. And while maintaining the values mentioned above surely gets us closer to accomplishing that goal, I'm a firm believer that showing is much better than telling. In other words, I've seen with my own two eyes how one of the most genuine and effective ways of passing our culture down to our children is to allow them to experience it firsthand by traveling to our own heritage country.

THERE'S NO PLACE LIKE HOME

By far, one of the most difficult parts of being an immigrant, at least for me, is being so far away from my extended family and *la tierra que me vio nacer.* Now that I'm raising my own children, this separation is also difficult because I know that, no matter what I do, my kids will never really get to experience a lot of the things from my culture that I so loved as a child. One the most important things is simply *la familia.*

My *abuelita,* who was born in 1914, is really old, but she's still doing well. She's hard of hearing, so calling her doesn't always go smoothly, but I still do it regularly just to hear her sweet voice—the voice all *abuelitas* should have. Without fail, every conversation goes something like this: she tells me she feels great, asks about the kids and my husband, and ALWAYS asks when we're going to visit her again. She misses me, she says. Then, she ends every conversation by reminding me she loves me and that she hopes all my dreams come true because I deserve nothing less. I cry, but silently because I don't want to make her sad. *Me hace tanta falta.*

But she's not the only one I miss dearly.

While I've spent the majority of my life in the United States and my immediate family is right here with me, I still have lots of family and friends back home in Peru. There's my favorite cousin, who is only nine months older than me, with whom I spent some of my best childhood years and whose children are very close in age to mine. There's my dad's entire side of the family, whom I love to visit because it makes me feel like he's still around and it allows me to give my children a glimpse of what he was like. Sadly, he died before they were born. Then, there's my mom's extended family on both of her parents' sides. Her father, my *abuelito,* had many brothers and sisters so there are many *tíos, tías* and *primos* to visit.

Although it's hard to believe, I've also managed to keep and nurture a few friendships from my childhood years in Lima. One of them in particular continues to be very strong, and it's a real treat to see our children play together whenever we visit.

While I rely heavily on photographs, videos and just simply storytelling to let my children know about our extended family back in Peru, I also make it a point for them to be as connected to them as possible to make sure we're keeping those bonds alive even from a distance. Luckily, gone are the days when making an international call was not only extremely costly, but pretty unreliable. Technology has advanced to the point where I can make sure my children are able to talk to and "see" their cousins by simply connecting to the Internet. Programs like Skype allow us all to feel a little closer to home, albeit in a virtual sort of way. And although I'm grateful for the existence of this technology, in our household, it's only one part of the equation. Another part of utmost importance is to actually create a sense within our children that both of their heritage countries—Peru and Puerto Rico—are also their homes.

A HOME AWAY FROM HOME

Home can be such a loaded word for an immigrant like myself. Depending on who asks it or what I'm trying to convey with my answer, the word can have many definitions. But, at the end of the day, nothing will ever make me feel like I'm back to my "real" home as much as landing at Jorge

Chavez International Airport in Lima, Peru, and getting a whiff of my beloved Pacific Ocean.

I had the opportunity to take my children back to Peru in 2011 and the experience was everything I'd hoped for and more. After clearing customs, I couldn't wait to be embraced by my loving family who was undoubtedly out there waiting for us, even though we arrived well after midnight. I knew my uncle—*mi padrino* and my mom's only brother—would be there, punctual as usual, standing among the crowd of people waiting impatiently until we locked eyes and he could breath easily again. I was finally home.

After the *besos y abrazos*, the introduction of the new family member—they hadn't met my son Santiago yet—the *"qué bien te ves"* y *"cuánto has crecido,"* we managed to get all our luggage and baby gear (traveling internationally with little ones is NO easy task!) into two cars and made our way to my abuelita's home, the only place that remains the same in the sea of constant change that is our lives. But first we made an obligatory stop at one of Lima's famed *pollerías* to get some Peruvian rotisserie chicken and a cold Inca Kola, my country's official drink, which is more popular than Coke.

In the days that followed, I made sure my children got to experience my homeland the way I had as a child. We spent lots of time at the same beach I'd gone to almost daily during the summer months. I took Vanessa to the school where I became bilingual and showed her my seventh grade classroom. I introduced both my children to the flavors of Peruvian cuisine, including *chicha morada*—a traditional Peruvian drink made of purple corn and one of my weaknesses—and was delighted when my daughter's eyes lit up after her first sip. The love affair had begun.

THE GOOD, THE BAD AND THE UGLY

Going to Peru was a treat for all of us in every sense. First, it was awesome to see my daughter interact in Spanish with other children when we were out and about. At the park, for example, she had no issues whatsoever. In fact, on one occasion when she saw a little girl playing on a see-saw with her dad and realized one of the seats was empty, she went up to them and asked: "*Señor, ¿puedo jugar con ustedes?*" I was very impressed.

I also loved that I got to share a bunch of stories with my daughter about my childhood in Lima. That's how we ended up eating a *vasito de lúcuma*—which is a small ice cream cup of vanilla and *lúcuma* (a fruit native to Peru). As soon as I heard the *heladero's* horn, I ran out to meet him like the child I once was, my daughter right behind me at the oceanside park where I spent many an afternoon when I was little.

While food was a huge part of our trip, the most gratifying part was seeing my children spend time with *la familia*. I truly enjoyed seeing my children interact with my almost centenarian *abuelita*. That part was priceless. Vanessa spent endless hours playing *en español* with her three cousins aged eleven, eight and three. There were no schedules, no rules, no curfews. It was all play, all day. My daughter would stay up late so she could play with her cousins, and I allowed it because their laughter was contagious (and because it took me back to a time when I used to do exactly the same thing with their parents, my cousins). If you'd have seen them, you would have thought they've grown up together when, in reality, they'd only seen each other three times in their lives!

But even with all the positives, I'd be lying if I said everything was perfect. Traveling to South America with small children can be daunting, especially if you've lived in the United States for a long time and you are used to things being done a certain way.

The first problem I always have is the issue of car seats. While I have no problem bringing them from the States, the reality is that, for the most part, we use taxis as a mode of transportation and, unfortunately, often they aren't even equipped with seat belts.

The other problem is the extremely high probability that someone in my family will get sick from the food they eat. (I, apparently, am exempt. I'm not sure if it's because I was born there and therefore have some kind of immunity to the bacteria that makes the others sick.) So while I want my family to experience the tastes of my country's cuisine, I'm also very careful as to what and where they eat. There's absolutely nothing fun about being sick and very far away from the comforts of home.

Finally, saying goodbye to my family is always extremely difficult because I never know how long it'll be before we see each other again. Without fail, there's lots of crying, hugs and well wishes. The last few hours are always pretty tense with anticipation of our looming departure and the hassle it can be to travel internationally with two small children.

Coming back to the States is also difficult because life here is so different on so many levels, from the taste of the food to the meaning of time. Our last trip back to the United States was hellish, to say the least. It took three planes to get from Lima to Denver. After missing our last connecting flight from Houston to Denver and just as I was about to *maldecir en silencio* the moment we decided to make such an unforgiving trip, Vanessa—who's obviously wiser than her much older mother—turned to me and said: "*Mami, gracias por llevarnos a tu país.*" She thanked me for taking them to my country!

If I wasn't sure before of the importance that exposure to our roots through traveling has on our bilingual and bicultural children, her genuine, unprompted comment cemented it. As one of the readers of our blog so eloquently put it, "this is the type of teaching that happens all on its own."

Traveling to both Peru and Puerto Rico is extremely expensive now that we're a family of four, especially when we can't stay longer than a couple of weeks due to our work commitments. But after seeing the impact this short trip to Peru had on our daughter, my husband and I have made a pact that traveling back home as often as possible—at least once a year to either country—has to be one of our priorities. I know that the bonds (family, culture, language) created during these trips will last a lifetime, but I want to make sure I continue nurturing them!

ANA SPEAKS OUT ABOUT HER DAUGHTER'S PRESCHOOL IMMERSION EXPERIENCE IN EL SALVADOR

THERE'S NO DOUBT IN MY MIND THAT THE MAIN REASON WHY I'M RAISING A bicultural daughter is because I want her to have a deep and real connection with her family, most of which lives in El Salvador and Mexico. My husband and I can certainly go to great lengths to fill the house with cultural traditions from both countries, read our daughter books about our countries, fill the air with sounds of our past and attend events which celebrate the rich traditions of our ancestors, but nothing at all beats the true immersion experience of traveling to our *familia's* homes and living life like a local would.

Though Camila is only five years old, shehas already been to El Salvador and Mexico three times each. We're lucky in the sense that, even though the trip itself is costly, we have family to stay with and very little expenses while we're there. Once we arrive, our priority really isn't to travel and visit places, it's just to assimilate to life in the country and enjoy the days as they come.

When my girl was three years old, the two of us spent a whole month in El Salvador. I was able to afford this luxury since I can carry my laptop and pretty much work from anywhere. My sister helped me place Camila in a local preschool so she could be completely immersed in Spanish and also entertained during the mornings when her beloved *prima* was in kindergarten.

I made the decision to enroll her in a local preschool for several reasons. First I wanted to strengthen her Spanish. I had a couple of friends who had done the same thing when they visited their families in Latin America and said their kids benefited from it. Also, even though we were away "on vacation," I had to continue working my part-time job from home. So, I needed to have some time alone to work.

My sister helped me find a preschool that was run by two friends who allowed Camila to come in for just one month. School starts in El Salvador the second week of August, right after a week-long national holiday known as *"Las Fiestas Patrias de Agosto."* Camila was able to be there on the first day of school, so that eased the transition a bit because the other kids were more welcoming to her being there, and she wasn't singled out as the "new girl."

It also helped a lot that, at that point in time, my daughter spoke mostly Spanish.

Camila really didn't have a hard time adapting to the actual school setting. I think it all happened so fast and so many new things, faces, foods and situations were thrown her way in a span of four weeks that she didn't have much time to react. She came back home to her *abuelita's* every day singing new songs in Spanish, talking more and more in complete sentences and mentioning names of new little *amigos*. The same little *amigos* created a card for her on her last day where they each put a print of their hands. She was so, so proud of it and still smiles when I read out the names on each hand to her.

Do I recommend this full immersion method in a new school and a new country to everyone? It depends. It can be a tough transition and a lot to assimilate at once. It's a method that worked for us because of my daughter's age (three years old), the timing (first day of school), the length of the visit (one month), my sister's help in finding the right place and Camila's fluency level in Spanish. If you have an adaptable child in the preschool years and a support system in the country you are visiting, then I absolutely recommend it.

During the preschool years children absorb all the information around them like sponges, especially language. A full immersion experience like this will cement the language foundation you're already building every day and will make the language even more relevant and special to your child. Not only that, but she will get to experience the day-to-day life of her heritage country firsthand and feel an unparalleled connection to it.

SUMMERS ABROAD

While my children are still too little, I can't wait until they're old enough to spend entire summers with either my family in Peru or my husband's family in Puerto Rico. We used to do this with my stepson, who's now a young man, and I can honestly say that those summer immersion trips are partly responsible for his bilingualism and biculturalism. Not only was he immersed in Spanish, but he also got to experience what living in Latin America is really like. Not to mention that he got to spend lots of quality time with his dad's side of the family, forging an unbreakable bond that I'm sure he'll continue to nurture.

I know we're very fortunate to have family in both countries willing to take on the responsibility of caring for our children for such an extended period of time. Thus, I plan on taking advantage of that opportunity without hesitation, even though I'm sure it'll be hard at first, as we'll all miss each other a lot. But my children are lucky to have many cousins close to their age and I'm sure they'll adapt quickly and the problem will then be that they won't want to come back to the States.

At first, the plan is for one of us to travel with them to help them settle in and set everything up. At the end of the summer, we'll travel back to pick them up and probably take some time off to spend with them and the rest of the family. When they get a bit older, though, we'll probably allow them to travel by themselves, just like we did with my stepson.

In spite of my own rocky summer camp immersion experience in the United States (see box on page 209), in an ideal world, I'd love to arrange for my children to get some sort of formal instruction in Spanish while they're there. Though I know having them experience everyday life will be extremely valuable, I think it'd be smart to also have them brush up on their writing and reading skills in Spanish.

MY ROCKY SUMMER CAMP EXPERIENCE

I REMEMBER IT LIKE IT WAS YESTERDAY, THE DREADFUL SUMMER CAMP WHERE my parents sent my little brother and I very soon after we arrived in Miami. It was a few weeks before school started and it was the most horrible thing I had to go through at the time. In retrospect, of course, it was truly an excellent idea on my parents' part. I can say this only now that I'm a mother myself, twenty-five years later. The truth is that by enrolling us in a summer camp my parents ensured that the transition into the public school system wasn't as difficult as it could have been, but that's not really the story I want to tell.

This is: my brother was barely ten, so he couldn't care less about any of this. But I was fourteen, and my dislike for my parents was endless. I was never really disobedient or disrespectful. But when we got to Miami, I wasn't too thrilled with my parents, to say the least. I hated everything about that stupid summer camp. I thought I was too old to be there. It seemed as if those who were my age were actually working there as camp counselors. I didn't like the American kids because even though I had spent years at a bilingual school in Peru, the truth is that I often didn't really understand what they were saying. I'd learned the proper way of speaking English at the excellent British private school I'd been privileged to attend back home, but nary a slang word used by American teenagers in the 1980s. I also hated not knowing how to dress. Having spent the majority of my childhood in private schools, wearing regular clothes to school was challenging, to put it lightly. I hated feeling like I didn't belong.

But I think what I hated the most was not knowing anything about American customs and traditions. I remember clearly that one of the events publicized at the summer camp was something called the Sadie Hawkins dance. As someone who'd just gotten off the "banana boat"—as the kids at school would later tell me in reference to the rafts used by Cuban immigrants in their perilous journey to Florida—I had absolutely no clue what Sadie Hawkins was and I wasn't about to ask any of the kids at camp for fear that I'd be ridiculed. (I can't help but think how much easier my life would've been if the Internet had existed back then!) I obviously couldn't ask my parents either because I was sure they would be even more lost.

Today, when I remember stuff like this, I'm convinced that not being able to relate to the music, movies, clothing and customs of the American kids of my generation was one of the most difficult aspects of being an immigrant—at least at the beginning. I'm not sure how this is going to play out for my children, but the plan—as we have put forward in this book—is to raise them to be both bilingual and bicultural so they feel comfortable in either of their cultures and don't have to go through the same awkward period as I did.

DISCOVERING A NEW CULTURE
BY TRAVELING ABROAD

I know this all sounds dreamy, but what if you have no family or friends back "home"? Or what if back "home" means Georgia and not a country in Latin America? Does that mean your children are to be excluded from experiencing what it is like to be immersed in our culture and language everywhere they turn?

Absolutely not. While it might be a little bit harder to plan, you can definitely give your children the full immersion experience by doing what some of the brave and adventurous readers of our blog have done.

Take Amy Conroy, for example, an anthropologist and a mother of three children she's raising to be bilingual, even though Spanish is not her first language. The creator of Habla Blah, Blah, a program that introduces children to Spanish through music, Amy realized that the best way to truly immerse her children in the Spanish language and the Latino culture was by temporarily moving to Mexico. In 2011 (and again in 2012), she did just that. For several months, she transplanted her family from Los Angeles to San Miguel de Allende, Mexico.

Through a series of posts Amy documented different aspects of her family's immersion experience, taking SpanglishBaby readers along for the ride.

"My husband and I made a pact early on in parenthood that we would only take our kids to Spanish-speaking countries given the opportunity... We didn't want them to learn another language in a void academic environment—I wanted them to understand the nuances of speech and words that don't translate directly. I wanted them to know that people laugh and cry and eat all over the world—but they do it differently and for many reasons. I wanted another language—and culture—to become 'normalized' to them," wrote Amy in her first post as an explanation of why she'd decided to make what many thought was a pretty radical decision.

Throughout the months of their experiment abroad, Amy's posts were honest and full of real life examples of what the experience was like for her children.

A lot of what she wrote had to do with the good parts of living in a place full of traditions and culture:

"I have never lived in such a celebratory environment in my life—the 'fiesta culture' here never stops! There are citywide parades and festivals all the time, fiestas and social gatherings for every reason, and children's birthday parties that joyfully extend well past bedtimes. Fireworks are an everyday all-the-time occurrence, which is not easy to imagine until you are woken at 4:30 am by a neighborhood celebration that started the day before… at 4 am… *los locos.*"

"And that's not even mentioning the birthday celebrations! We love the piñatas, the '*Dale Dale*' song, and *cascarones,* but our favorite birthday tradition is a new one we've been introduced to: '*Mordidita! mordidita!*' is chanted all around after the candles are blown out. It's the prompt for the birthday person's head to be smashed into the center of the cake by a loving party-goer who is perfectly positioned for the task. We were lucky enough to have been invited to the party by a very spirited mover-and-shaker who wasn't waiting for the prod. Totally surprising us AND the whole party, the newest little five-year-old on the block smashed his own face into his cake, filling it with frosting like a clown in a pie contest. It was awesome! Hilarious! And stunning.

214

Immediately my five-year-old declared, 'I'm going to do that, too, when it's my birthday!' I love this culture. These people know how to celebrate life."

But not all was celebration. Amy also described some of their difficulties adapting to a new (temporary) life far away from all that's known.

"We've been here a month, and it happened—Jack hit 'the wall'. Sadly but somewhat predictably, my oldest had his first break with cultural assimilation.

We had been watching the sunset with a gorgeous and captivating vista, eating scrumptious food, celebrating our family's Easter visit, and it all came together—or you could say, fell apart. He missed home. He missed Daddy. He missed his friends, his toys, everything. I totally understood where he was coming from—everything here is different. He is adapting beautifully, but you'd need to lack memory to not miss the things that make you feel comfortable."

Amy also pointed out the everyday differences between the United States and Mexico.

"Whatever you think is going to be easy, most likely isn't. Conversely, whatever you anticipate being difficult might just be easy. I have lots of examples to share.

Enrolling in school? Tedious at home (U.S.) and filled with applications and wait lists, but super easy here—done in a day. Joining a Country Club? Fill out an application and pay money in the United States. Here? Additionally, please provide us with copies of your marriage certificate, birth certificates, and felony record if applicable. Fresh fruit juice? Dime a dozen here vs. costly at home. Phone call? All depends on the resources available and how well you understand the cellular vs. landline infrastructure of Mexico, i.e. can easily be confusing. Transportation? We hop in our car to go anywhere

215

at home. Here, you walk, which I LOVE, or you take a taxi for twenty five *pesos* nearly everywhere. Parking is considered unmanageable, so you're better off not having to deal with a car."

Amy's series of posts, entitled "An Immersion Adventure in Mexico" was pretty popular. The readers who followed her family's adventure not only made comments, but some of them also had a lot of questions, proving that there's a lot of interest in doing something similar from other parents raising bilingual and bicultural children.

SUSAN'S FAMILY STUDY ABROAD EXPERIENCE IN PERU

I GET A BIT JEALOUS WHEN I READ ABOUT OTHER PEOPLE'S TRAVELS TO VISIT family in Spanish-speaking countries. What a great way to not only connect with family, but also to reinforce the Spanish being taught at home in the United States. Unfortunately, I don't have family abroad to visit, but I was convinced that my own children would greatly benefit from the experience of visiting another country and being immersed in Spanish.

Back in high school I started studying Spanish, but it was during a semester study abroad program in Spain that I actually achieved fluency. There is nothing like being completely immersed in the language to learn how to speak it with confidence and ease.

For our family study abroad experience, I chose Peru. My husband and I had traveled throughout Peru prior to having children and just fell in love with the country, its culture and people. Before our sons were born, we rarely planned our trips, having only a rough itinerary and our plane tickets. Traveling with children changed my usual travel style, so I started planning our trip eight months prior to our departure. I began to research different schools and programs so that our whole family could spend time immersed in Spanish and the culture of Peru. My plan was to duplicate many aspects of my own study abroad adventure, and I was able to achieve a similar experience for our entire family.

My sons both spoke Spanish well before our trip, but now they are experts. We spent a month living in Arequipa with our home stay family. Living with a Peruvian family was a rewarding experience, and we were fortunate to have been placed with a family that was friendly, welcoming and supportive. Our host mother Marta went out of her way to help us feel welcome and at home.

Living day to day completely surrounded by Spanish was wonderful. My sons were also fortunate to have had lots of opportunities to play in Spanish with other children, too. We were able to visit a preschool to play with other children, and the grandchildren of our host family were always coming over to play.

Originally I had planned to put the boys into a preschool program, but my son's bilingual preschool teacher suggested private classes instead since it typically takes children a month to adjust to a new preschool. Fortunately, I found a school that had teachers who specialized in teaching young children. The situation was perfect. My husband and I took Spanish classes while our sons were each taking classes with their own teacher. My older son was being taught to read using the Coquito method, which is a Peruvian method of teaching that I think is one of the best in the world. My younger son spent a lot of time singing, reading and just playing with his teacher in Spanish. The boys' teachers were wonderful, and for two hours a day, I was able to work with my own teacher studying Peruvian literature and furthering my own language skills.

We also traveled while in Peru to expose the boys to more than just life in the city. We spent time visiting an ancient religious site of the Wari Civilization and seeing the Inca terraces and small villages of the Colca Canyon. I was pleased that my sons loved to travel as much as their father and I do.

This trip has been a wonderful experience for our entire family. My husband and I plan to use Spanish with each other so that he will not lose the fluency he acquired while living abroad. As a non-native speaker raising bilingual children, I am more confident in my own abilities and am inspired to continue reading in Spanish to further my own language skills. Most importantly, living in Peru was a wonderful experience for my own children. Being immersed in the language has really helped develop their Spanish, and their traveling and playing with Peruvian children is helping them become citizens of the world.

I highly recommend this experience to other families.

BONUS TIPS FOR TRAVELING BILINGUAL FAMILIES

FOUR REASONS WHY TRAVELING IS SO IMPORTANT WHEN RAISING BILINGUAL AND BICULTURAL CHILDREN

1) **Full time exposure to Spanish.** I once wrote about how I inadvertently found out Vanessa plays in English because this area of her life is mostly covered by English while she is in school. While in Peru, I pretty much let Vanessa play, play and play some more with her three cousins. And because of that her "play" vocabulary expanded exponentially! She also figured out that while we all speak Spanish, there are many variations of the language, a topic I've written about extensively on the blog. For some unknown reason (I mean, I have an idea of the history behind it, but it still doesn't make sense), Peruvians call birthdays *santos* instead of *cumpleaños*. And since we got to celebrate both my *ahijado*'s and my birthday the last time we were in Peru, Vanessa heard this word over and over again until she finally asked me what it was.

2) **Showing them our culture is way better than telling them about it.** Culture entails many things, including language, food, music, traditions and, in the case of Latinos, *familia*. Instead of telling my daughter about all these, she got to experience it all firsthand and I was thrilled to see she loved every aspect of it. From our very, very loud family reunions to the two days we spent at the beach doing what I always did as child there: nothing.

3) **A chance to stock up on all things Spanish.** Before I had kids, I used to spend tons of money at the bookstore whenever I traveled to Peru, or any other Spanish-speaking

country, for that matter. While Amazon has gotten better and better in terms of their Spanish language selection, still nothing beats browsing the aisles of a bookstore in search of that perfect book you've been dying to read. No more. Now I do the same thing but for children's books in Spanish. There's an amazing bookstore just three blocks from my grandmother's apartment, so it was one of the first places we visited! Vanessa was in heaven. I spent a fortune, but I left with four bags full of books and music for her and her brother. The kind of stuff I'll never be able to get on Amazon.

4) **An opportunity to expand their horizons and to see how life is different but also the same in other parts of the world.** Again, the only way to truly understand this is to live it, albeit for a short period of time. I think that one important take-away for my daughter was seeing why it's important to speak Spanish and how this is a language spoken in many other countries around the world. I hope I never have to do it, but I know that reminding her of how she had no problems communicating with anybody there will serve as a strong detractor if she ever refuses to speak Spanish!

TRAVELING INTERNATIONALLY
WITH SMALL CHILDREN

If you've traveled anywhere with your children—even if it was a trip to your local camping site for the weekend—you already know that one of the most important things is to pack enough activities and snacks to last through three of the same trips! But here are some very important tips to consider when you go overseas:

- **Passports:** Take care of this one as soon as possible. Although the actual process is not too difficult, it does take some time—unless you don't care to pay a hefty fee to expedite it. Also, make photocopies of everybody's passports. Take one set of copies with you and leave the other set with someone staying behind. Better to be safe than sorry.
- **Vaccines:** There are different immunization recommendations depending on each country. The Center for Disease Control has a list on a country by country basis, so go check it before you travel or consult your doctor.
- **Carry-on:** Pack what each of your children need to survive for a whole day in case your checked luggage gets lost or delayed. Believe me, it happens all the time. Ideally, each child should have her own carry-on.
- **Milk:** Not all planes carry milk and I found this one out the hard way. I still don't know how this is even possible, but to avoid future disasters, I now make it a point to purchase milk once we've cleared security.
- **Stroller & baby carrier:** When deciding which one to bring, I say both. At the airport, there's nothing worse than having to take the baby out of the stroller at the security check point, so put him in baby carrier instead. However, strollers are a godsend during long layovers.
- **Electronics:** Be aware that not all countries have the same electrical plugs and voltage. When we travel to Peru, for example, we always make sure to take adapters since

the voltage is 220 V compared to the 110 V in the United States.

- **Portable high chair:** Although it's hard to believe, not every establishment overseas has high chairs readily available for our children. I also found this one out the hard way. So, if your child still uses a high chair, I suggest you get a portable one and avoid the hassle.
- **Medication:** You'll probably be able to find the same or similar over-the-counter children's medications, but if you absolutely want to use what your kids are used to, bring your own.

Of course, not every family has the financial means—or the courage—to jump into such an invaluable experience. Even so, there are other options to be considered, especially when it comes to older children. My parents, for example, sent my sister to the United States as a teenager through a student exchange program so that she could solidify her English skills and get to experience how Americans live. I've always thought my parents were ahead of their time and this is just one more example of that. My sister spent three months in Tampa, Florida, immersed in the English language and the American culture and, to this day, she attributes that experience to her ability to adapt so quickly once we moved from Peru to the United States when she was eighteen.

"My short experience as an exchange student in the United States was something that I will never forget. Simply put, it was a breath of fresh air. I can't thank my parents enough for being so open-minded and giving me the chance to learn about another culture, one that today I consider my own," my sister, Gloria, wrote about her student exchange experience in a guest post for SpanglishBaby.

Yes, my sibling and I were very lucky to have forward-thinking parents who believed it was important for us to learn about other cultures and languages. But, they also instilled in us a love for all things Peruvian as they raised us far away from our homeland. For that, I'll be forever grateful. I plan on doing the same for my kids—even though Peru is only one part of their heritage.

Afterword

✳

S PANGLISHBABY WAS BORN IN FEBRUARY 2009 BECAUSE BOTH Ana and I realized that, like us, most Latina moms (regardless of their level of acculturation) want to pass on our culture, heritage, language and traditions to our *niños*, but we don't always know how. Within a few months of launching our blog, we also realized that Latino parents weren't the only ones interested in raising bilingual children, since many of our readers—as presented throughout this book—are not only monolingual, but they have absolutely no connection to the Latino culture other than some sort of attraction and a driving desire to make sure their children learn the second most spoken language in the world.

We like to think we're putting *nuestro granito de arena* towards making that goal a reality. While there will be many times along the way when you might get discouraged by your children's rebellion when it comes to using the minority language or what seems to be a lack of progression in terms of their Spanish vocabulary, please don't give up and always know that you're not alone. In fact, there's a bilingual parenting revolution going on right now. All you need to do is read through the chapters in this book or visit SpanglishBaby.com to actively participate in this community and get the reassurance you're looking for so that you don't feel left out. If you're looking for even more guidance, you can also check out our Resources chapter where you'll find a plethora of information to help you as you traverse the sometimes difficult, but highly rewarding journey of raising bilingual and bicultural children. And, if all else fails, you can always turn to this fittingly beautiful Czech proverb, "Learn a new language and get a new soul."

Resources

＊

SPANGLISHBABY WAS CREATED AS A COMMUNITY SITE WHERE parents can feel confident they will get the latest information, advice and tips about raising bilingual and bicultural children. Since the day we launched in 2009 we've been developing a "Resources" section—one of the most popular areas of SpanglishBaby.com—where we've compiled a long list of useful links on all sorts of bilingual matters pertaining to children and parenting, organized into tidy categories to help readers find exactly what they need.

In this chapter, we've included a comprehensive list of sites for information regarding bilingual education, bilingual parenting communities, sites with more resources and even bonus tips for helping you raise bilingual and bicultural children.

We've tried our best to provide the most up to date information possible since we know how valuable it is for time-crunched parents who need to find useful information in one place. If you feel we've missed a resource that is helpful to you and we should all know about, please send us a message via the blog so we can review it for addition.

BILINGUAL EDUCATION

The sites below (in alphabetical order) are a great starting point for parents researching the bilingual education path:

CENTER FOR APPLIED LINGUISTICS (CAL)–Dedicated to providing a comprehensive range of research-based information, tools and resources related to language and culture.	 www.cal.org/
CENTER FOR ADVANCED RESEARCH ON LANGUAGE ACQUISITION (CARLA)–is one of the U.S. Department of Education's Title VI National Language Resource Centers, whose role is to improve the nation's capacity to teach and learn foreign languages effectively.	 http://carla.umn.edu/
CENTER FOR MULTILINGUAL MULTICULTURAL RESEARCH–an organized research unit at the University of Southern California. Interests include: "language and literacy acquisition; bilingualism and biliteracy; language proficiency testing; integrating language and content instruction in the classroom..." and more. (Site provides a resource page.)	 www.usc.edu/dept/ education/CMMR/

DIRECTORY OF FOREIGN LANGUAGE IMMERSION PROGRAMS IN U.S. SCHOOLS–CAL's searchable directory of language immersion programs. This directory includes elementary, middle, and high schools that teach all or part of their curriculum through a second language. Such programs are referred to as total or partial immersion programs. In general, the programs are designed for students whose native language is English.	 www.cal.org/resources/immersion/
DIRECTORY OF TWO-WAY BILINGUAL IMMERSION PROGRAMS IN THE U.S.–Maintained by the Center for Applied Linguistics (CAL). The directory was last updated December 3, 2010 and lists 384 programs in 28 states (plus D.C.)	 www.cal.org/twi/directory/
EDUTOPIA–Home to The George Lucas Educational Foundation, Edutopia's mission is to "spread the word about ideal, interactive learning environments and enable others to adapt these successes locally." http://www.edutopia.org/	 www.edutopia.org/
HERITAGE LANGUAGES IN AMERICA–The Alliance for the Advancement of Heritage Languages is committed to advancing language development for heritage language speakers in the United States as part of a larger effort to educate members of our society who can function professionally in English and in other languages.	 www.cal.org/heritage/index.html

NATIONAL ASSOCIATION FOR BILINGUAL EDUCATION (NABE)–National professional organization devoted to representing Bilingual Learners and Bilingual Education professionals.	 www.nabe.org/index.html
NATIONAL CLEARINGHOUSE FOR ENGLISH LANGUAGE ACQUISITION AND LANGUAGE INSTRUCTION EDUCATIONAL PROGRAMS–Collects, coordinates and conveys a broad range of research and resources in support of an inclusive approach to high quality education for English Language Learners (ELLs).	 www.ncela.gwu.edu/
NATIONAL COALITION FOR PARENT INVOLVEMENT IN EDUCATION–Building family-school partnerships that work.	 www.ncpie.org/
ÑANDUTÍ–comprehensive resource on foreign language teaching and learning in grades preK-8. Based on the premise that learning another language is beneficial and that students of all ages can learn a language.	 www.cal.org/earlylang/

THE NATIONAL NETWORK FOR EARLY LANGUAGE LEARNING–an educational community providing leadership in support of successful early language learning and teaching.	 http://nnell.org/

And, of course, **SPANGLISHBABY'S** BILINGUAL EDUCATION directory–A user-generated and searchable directory of immersion programs ranging from daycares to high schools.

http://spanglishbaby.com/
category/bilingual-education/

BILINGUAL RESOURCES

A list of sites that offer interesting reads, forums and/or products for parents raising bilingual children.

BabyCenter en español	http://espanol.babycenter.com/
The Bilingual Family Newsletter	www.bilingualfamilynewsletter.com/
Bilingual Fun	www.bilingualfun.com/
Boca Beth	www.bocabeth.com/

Colorín Colorado	 http://colorincolorado.org/
Discovery Familia	 www.eslpartyland.com/
Foreign Language Fun	 http://foreignlanguagefun.com/
Fun For Spanish Teachers	 http://funforspanishteachers. blogspot.com/
Fun French and Spanish	 www.fun-french-and-spanish.com/ index.html

Habla blah blah	http://hablablahblah.com/
Hispanic Culture Online	www.hispanic-culture-online.com/ spanish-for-kids.html
InCultureParent	www.incultureparent.com/
Latin Baby Book Club	www.latinbabybookclub.com/
Learning the Language	http://blogs.edweek.org/edweek/ learning-the-language/

Little Pim	www.littlepim.com/
Mis Cositas	www.miscositas.com/
Mommy Maestra	www.mommymaestra.com
Multilingual Living	www.multilingualliving.com/
Multilingual Mania	http://multilingualmania.com/

Nuestros Niños	www.nuestrosninos.com/
Online Free Spanish	www.onlinefreespanish.com/
Psychology Today	www.psychologytoday.com/blog/ life-bilingua
Spanish Playground	www.spanishplayground.net/
Todo Bebé	www.todobebe.com/

At the **BILINGUAL READERS** website, you can also find a wide range of resources on bilingualism, early literacy and language acquisition.

www.bilingualreaders.com

BILINGUAL COMMUNITIES

Bilingual Families Connect	www.bilingualfamiliesconnect.com/
Bilingual/Bicultural Family Network	www.biculturalfamily.org/
Bilingualism Matters	www.bilingualism-matters.org.uk/
Bilingual Parenting in a Foreign Language	http://humanities.byu.edu/bilingua/
Center for Research on Bilingualism in Theory & Practice	www.bilingualism.bangor.ac.uk/

Multilingual Children's Association	
	www.multilingualchildren.org/

OTHER WAYS TO KEEP
OUR LATINO CULTURE ALIVE

Music: If there's one thing Latinos know how to do, it's how to party! And we have all the genres of music to do so. Music has been a part of my life for as long as I can remember, and when I met my Puerto Rican husband, my love for it solidified. He's taught me a lot not only about classic salsa, but also about bomba and plena, among others. It's no wonder that as soon as our children hear a Latin beat, they break out in dance.

The most awesome part about music is that you don't really have to put too much effort into it. You can just turn on the radio, use Pandora, or even YouTube to find a ton of really great music in Spanish. Hit play and let the beats go on. If you know the words to the songs, go ahead and sing. Dancing is optional, but is always a blast—not to mention a stress reliever.

Another option is to make it a point to try to learn more about a specific musician or genre. This can be especially useful and fun if you have children because not only can both of you learn something new, but it'll show your kids how much you truly value your Latino culture.

Traditions/Cultural Events: Speaking of traditions, there is no better way to hold on to our heritage than to celebrate our cultural *costumbres*. No matter where your family hails from, there are sure to be tons of traditions celebrated in any given month. From your country of origin's independence day to *Día de Muertos*, take advantage of these celebrations to honor your Latino heritage.

If you're not too sure about these traditions and you're lucky enough to live where there's a big Latino population, check out what kind of public festivities there are in your area and try to make it to one of them. I promise it'll be fun. You can either do a search online or check the calendar of events in your local Spanish weekly. Museums and libraries are pretty good about putting together cultural events for the community, including story time, lectures, exhibitions and concerts.

Even if you live far away from anything Latino, you can still celebrate our traditions on your own. Do some research online to find out more about the specific tradition you'd like to celebrate to get ideas about some of the things you could do at home. You can find tons of ideas for activities, suggested reading lists, and even recipes for many of the more popular Latino celebrations, including *Día de Muertos*, *Noche Buena* and *Día de Reyes* on SpanglishBaby.com.

Bibliography

*

Chapter 1

Grace Flores-Hughes Interview—She Made "Hispanic" Official, Sunday, July 26, 2009, The Washington Post, viewed 15 September 2011, <http://www.washingtonpost.com/wp-dyn/content/article/2009/07/24/AR2009072402091_pf.html>

ENNIS, S.R.; RIOS-VARGAS, M., & ALBERT, N.G., *The Hispanic Population: 2010*, United States 2010 Census, viewed 14 October 2011, <http://www.census.gov/prod/cen2010/briefs/c2010br-04.pdf>

TAYLOR, P.; LOPEZ, M.H.; MARTÍNEZ, J.H., & VELASCO, G., *When Labels Don't Fit: Hispanics and Their Views of Identity*, Pew Hispanic Center, Wednesday April 4, 2012, <http://http://www.pewhispanic.org/files/2012/04/PHC-Hispanic-Identity.pdf>

State of the Hispanic Consumer: The Hispanic Market Imperative, Nielsen, Quarter 2, 2012, <http://nielsen.com//content/dam/corporate/us/en/reports-downloads/2012-Reports/State-of-the-Hispanic-Consumer.pdf>

Chapter 2

BARAC, R., & BIALYSTOK, E. (2012). *Bilingual Effects on Cognitive and Linguistic Development: Role of Language, Cultural Background, and Education,* Child Development, 83: 413–422, viewed 8 February 2012, <http://onlinelibrary.wiley.com/doi/10.1111/j.1467-8624.2011.01707.x/abstract?globalMessage=0>

BHATTACHARJEE, Y. (2012). *Why Bilinguals Are Smarter,* New York: The New York Times, viewed 17 March 2012, <http://www.nytimes.com/2012/03/18/opinion/sunday/the-benefits-of-bilingualism.html?_r=2&ref=opinion>

BIALYSTOK, E. (2011). *Coordination of Executive Functions in Monolingual and Bilingual Children,* Journal of Experimental Child Psychology, 110: 461-468, viewed 30 November 2011<http://www.sciencedirect.com/science/article/pii/S0022096511001330>

DREIFUS, C. (2011). *The Bilingual Advantage,* New York: The New York Times, viewed 1 June 2011, <http://www.nytimes.com/2011/05/31/science/31conversation.html>

GARCIA-SIERRA, A.; RIVERA-GAXIOLA, M.; CONBOY, B.T.; ROMO, H.; PERCACCIO, C. R.; KLARMAN, L.; ORTIZ, S., & KUHL, P. K. (2011). *Socio-cultural Environment and Bilingual Language Learning: A Longitudinal Event Related Potential Study,* Journal of Phonetics, 39: 456-557, viewed 15 November 2011, <http://www.sciencedirect.com/science/article/pii/S0095447011000660>

KAUSHANSKAYA, M., & MARIAN, V. (2011). *The Bilingual Advantage in Novel Word Learning,* Psychonomic Bulletin and Review, viewed 5 February 2012, <http://www.comdis.wisc.edu/research/LABlab/docs/1_K&M_2009%20PBR.pdf>

LUST, B. & YANG, S. (2009). *Discovering Child Language*

and Cognitive Growth, Cornell University, viewed 20 October 2011, <http://www.human.cornell.edu/hd/outreach-extension/loader.cfm?csModule=security/getfile&PageID=43544>

PEARSON, B.Z. (2008). *Raising a Bilingual Child,* New York: Living Language.

POULIN-DUBOIS; D., BLAYE, A.; COUTYA, J., & BIALYSTOK, E. (2011). *The Effects of Bilingualism on Toddlers' Executive Functioning,* Journal of Experimental Child Psychology, 108: 567-579, viewed 22 January 2012, <http://www.sciencedirect.com/science/article/pii/S0022096510002079>

ROMO, H. (2007). *The Bilingual Baby Project,* University of Texas at San Antonio, viewed 5 January, 2012, <http://www.utsa.edu/discovery/2007/f_baby_p1.htm>

VAN ASSCHE, E.; DUYCK, W.; HARTSUIKER, R., & DIEPENDAELE, K. (2009). *Does Bilingualism Change Native-Language Reading? Cognate Effects in a Sentence Context,* Psychological Science, viewed 28 November 2011, <http://www.psychologicalscience.org/media/releases/2009/vanassche.cfm>

WERKER, J. (2010). *The Roots of Bilingualism in Newborns,* Association for Psychological Science, viewed 25 November 2011, <http://www.psychologicalscience.org/media/releases/2010/werker.cfm>

Chapter 3

PEARSON, B.Z. (2008). *Raising a Bilingual Child,* New York: Living Language.

KESTER, E.S. (2011). *Ask An Expert: How do I build proficiency in my non-native language to help my child become bilingual?*, SpanglishBaby, <http://spanglishbaby.com/ask-an-expert/ask-an-expert-how-do-i-build-proficiency-in-my-non-native-language-to-help-my-child-become-bilingual/>

Chapter 4

BAKER, C. (1997). *Foundations of Bilingual Education and Bilingualism*, 2nd Ed., New York: Multilingual Matters, pp. 213-215.

COLLIER, V.P., & THOMAS, W.P. (2004). *The Astounding Effectiveness of Dual Language Education for All*, abstract, viewed 11 February 2012, <http://njrp.tamu.edu/2004/PDFs/Collier.pdf>

DE VILLAR, R.A., FALTIS, C.J., & CUMMINS, J.P. (1994). *Cultural Diversity in Schools: From Rhetoric to Practice*, New York: State University of New York Press

ENNIS, S.R.; RIOS-VARGAS, M., & ALBERT, N.G., *The Hispanic Population: 2010*, United States 2010 Census, viewed 28 December 2011, <http://www.census.gov/prod/cen2010/briefs/c2010br-04.pdf>

GOLD, N. (2010). *Bilingual Schools Make Exceptional Gains on the State's Academic Performance Index (API)*, Californians Together: A Roundtable for Quality Education, viewed 15 January 2012, <http://www.usc.edu/dept/education/CMMR/NEWS/API_Report_Full.pdf>

KRISTOFF, N. (2010). *Hay Que Aprender Español. Ranhou Zai Xue Zhongwen* (First Learn Spanish. Then Study Chinese.), New York: The New York Times, viewed 20 December 2011, <http://www.nytimes.com/2010/12/30/opinion/30kristof.html>

LINDHOLM-LEARY, K. (2000). *Biliteracy for a Global Society:*

An Idea Book On Dual Language Education, Washington, DC: The George Washington University, viewed 2 March 2012, <www.ncela.gwu.edu/files/uploads/9/BiliteracyForAGlobalSociety.pdf>

McGrath, M. (2010). *The History of Bilingual Education As a Civil Right in the United States-Part One,* Multilingual Mania, viewed 25 June 2010, <http://multilingual-mania.com/the-history-of-bilingual-education-as-a-civil-right-in-the-united-states-part-one/>

Suárez-Orozco, C. & Suárez-Orozco, M. (2009). *The Best Ways to Teach Young Newcomers,* New York: The New York Times, viewed 25 March 2009, <http://roomforde-bate.blogs.nytimes.com/2009/03/11/the-best-ways-to-teach-young-newcomers/#orozco>

The Mexican-American Boom: Births Overtake Immigration, 2011, Pew Hispanic Center, viewed 18 July 2011, <http://www.pewhispanic.org/2011/07/14/the-mexican-american-boom-brbirths-overtake-immigration/>

Chapter 5

Alphonso, C. (2011). *Bilingual Acquisition Begins in Utero, Study Finds,* The Globe and Mail, viewed 28 February 2011 <http://www.theglobeandmail.com/news/technology/science/bilingual-acquisition-begins-in-utero-study-finds/article1470649/>

BabyCenter® Releases Acculturation Study About Latina Moms, 2011, PRNewswire, viewed 21 February 2011, <http://www.prnewswire.com/news-releases/babycenter-releases-acculturation-study-about-latina-moms-116153729.html>

Between Two Worlds: How Young Latinos Come of Age in America, 2009, Pew Hispanic Center, viewed 15 December 2009, <http://www.pewhispanic.org/2009/12/11/between-two-worlds-how-young-latinos-come-of-age-in-america/>

CITRIN, J.; LERMAN, A.; MURAKAMI, M., & PEARSON K. (2007). *Testing Huntington: Is Hispanic Immigration a Threat to American Identity?,* American Political Science Association, viewed 8 April 2007, <http://www.apsanet.org/imgtest/PerspectivesMar07Citrin_etal.pdf>

GROSJEAN, F. (2011). *How Cultures Combine and Blend in a Person,* Psychology Today, viewed 25 March 2011, <http://www.psychologytoday.com/blog/life-bilingual/201105/how-cultures-combine-and-blend-in-person>

HAKIMZADEH, S., & COHN, D. (2007). *English Usage Among Hispanics in the United States,* Pew Hispanic Center, viewed 30 November 2010, <http://www.pewhispanic.org/2007/11/29/english-usage-among-hispanics-in-the-united-states/>

PEARSON, B.Z. (2008). *Raising a Bilingual Child,* New York: Living Language.

Chapter 6

BabyCenter® Releases Acculturation Study About Latina Moms, 2011, PRNewswire, viewed 21 February 2011, <http://www.prnewswire.com/news-releases/babycenter-releases-acculturation-study-about-latina-moms-116153729.html>

CONROY, A. (2011). *One Family's Total Immersion Adventure in Mexico,* SpanglishBaby, <http://spanglishbaby.com/2011/04/one-familys-total-immersion-adventure-in-mexico/>